The Elements of Voice First Style
A Practical Guide to Voice User Interface Design

Ahmed Bouzid and Weiye Ma

Beijing · Boston · Farnham · Sebastopol · Tokyo

The Elements of Voice First Style

by Ahmed Bouzid and Weiye Ma

Published by O'Reilly Media, Inc., 1005 Gravenstein Highway North, Sebastopol, CA 95472.

O'Reilly books may be purchased for educational, business, or sales promotional use. Online editions are also available for most titles (*http://oreilly.com*). For more information, contact our corporate/institutional sales department: 800-998-9938 or *corporate@oreilly.com*.

Acquisitions Editor: Amanda Quinn	**Indexer:** Ellen Troutman-Zaig
Development Editor: Jill Leonard	**Interior Designer:** David Futato
Production Editor: Kate Galloway	**Cover Designer:** Karen Montgomery
Copyeditor: nSight, Inc.	**Illustrator:** Kate Dullea
Proofreader: Amnet Systems LLC	

May 2022:   First Edition

Revision History for the First Edition
          2022-05-16:   First Release

See   *http://oreilly.com/catalog/errata.csp?isbn=9781098119591*   for   release details.

978-1-098-11959-1

[LSI]

Praise for The Elements of Voice First Style

Rare is a book that can teach beginners and experts
so deeply and practically. These lessons will grow
alongside voice technology for years to come.

—*Julia Anderson, conversation designer & writer*

You knew the What, now here's the detailed step-by-step
"How to do Conversation Design." A first!

—*Maria Aretoulaki, principal consultant CX
design (voice & conversational AI) at GlobalLogic
and director at DialogCONNECTION*

The Elements of Voice First Style establishes the foundations
for a new wave of applications designed to truly delight users.
Fortunately, technology has finally enabled the nuance and
sophistication that Bouzid and Ma so artfully postulate.

—*Corey Miller, ASR research manager at Rev.com*

As a long-time specialist in conversational technologies, I've
often asked how the principles espoused in *The Elements of Style*,
the venerated writers' guide by William Strunk, Jr., and E.B.
White, could be adopted by designers of voicebots and "Voice
First" applications. This practical guide by Bouzid and Ma is
the answer to that question. It is an homage to Strunk and
White that provides a very accessible, yet comprehensive set of
guidelines for aspiring designers for intelligent voice assistants.

—*Dan Miller, founder of Opus Research*

The Elements of Voice First Style: A Practical Guide to Voice User Interface Design is informative, brilliant, and a must read for those in the industry to those wanting to learn from the best!

—*Audrey Arbeeny, CEO/founder/executive producer at Audiobrain*

The book offers precious voicebot design best practices!

—*Giorgio Robino, conversational AI technical leader at Almawave.it*

If you are building voice-based apps, this book is a must read. It shares the essential fundamentals for beginners and practical guidance for experts who are interested in gaining a deeper understanding of building high quality voicebots.

—*Rajiv Bammi, senior engineering leader*

Voice first technology needs honest perspectives to show the way forward. Ahmed and Weiye's book provides exactly that; new ways to think about old problems, how to make improvements, when voice isn't a good solution, and what's wrong with the status quo. Burst the hype bubble—read this book!

—*Benjamin McCulloch, conversation designer (with audio super powers)*

To our parents.

Table of Contents

Preface

This book has been almost twenty years in the making. During those years, the running line among practitioners in the speech technology field was, and for many still remains: "Speech is just around the corner." Meaning, by this time next year, God willing, speech technology will finally deliver on its promise and at long last be adopted as a reliable way for humans to retrieve and create information, as well as do other things; instead of typing, pushing buttons, tapping and swapping, they will just speak and listen.

In the early days, the proposition that "Speech is just around the corner" was an earnest aspiration. There was exuberance (this was the 1990s after all) and, for the most part, the prediction was hope-filled. In hindsight, the proposition looks almost irrational, given the state of the technology's usability at the time, its cost, and its basic performance (slow and inaccurate). But then, as the years wore on, the prediction turned into a healthy mix of self-deprecation ("How could we have been so arrogant?"), stubborn defiance ("But, we *will* make it happen!"), and a sober aversion to anything that smacks of hype ("And when it does seem to be happening, we will keep our skeptical eyes wide open").

In voice telephony systems, otherwise known as the unloved *interactive voice response* (IVR) applications, humans call a phone number intending to speak to another human only to be unpleasantly met by a system that tries to speak and listen. Those were the first interactive speech technologies deployed for mainstream use and eventually did go mainstream in the early 2000s. And although they did deliver undeniable value, notwithstanding the justified grousing from users, they somehow didn't count as the fulfillment of the "speech is just around the corner" aspiration. It was not until the launch of the iPhone 4S on October 4, 2011 (one day before the death of Steve Jobs), that one could arguably say that speech had arrived: Siri was born and interactive speech was now available, on demand, for the tens of millions of people who owned an iPhone at the time.

The arrival of Siri was a watershed moment not only because interactive speech was now available on a smartphone, but also because the type of speech-based interactions that it delivered were fundamentally different from the ones that users were encountering in IVR systems. The key difference lies in the fact that when someone calls a phone number, they usually want to speak with a human being, and when they encounter an automated system instead, they have to decide whether or not they want to interact, immediately ask for an agent (or "zero-out"), or hang up. With Siri, in contrast, the user is *willingly* engaging in self-service speech automation. When they press and hold the home button (as the first interactions with Siri had the user do), they are not expecting to speak to a human; they *expect* and *want* to speak to the speech app. In other words, the user wants to self-serve using speech and is not intending to speak to a human. This was a first for mainstream interactive voice technology.

Even so, Siri never really took off the way we speech practitioners were hoping it would. After the initial swell of enthusiasm, it quickly became clear that what we had witnessed with Siri was not the fulfillment of "speech is just around the corner" but rather an incremental, though important, enhancement of a multimodal interface to which a new mode—voice—was added. Not only could you see, touch, and feel (through haptic responses), but you could also speak and listen to fulfill self-service tasks. Siri did, however, achieve a major accomplishment for which we speech practitioners should forever be thankful to Steve Jobs: it introduced a cutting-edge, "cool" context within which speech was being used—namely the iPhone—raising the brand standing of speech as a technology that now had a future to look forward to beyond the crabbed and unexciting world of telephony IVR.

And so, we had to wait for November 8, 2014, when Amazon Echo arrived to be able to make a reasonable case that speech was no longer just around the corner but that it had made the turn.

Amazon Echo was the first device to deliver on three fundamental aspects of the voice interface that made it a candidate for fulfilling the promise of speech technology. (1) Like Siri, it was an interface where the user engaged the speech system willingly but—and this is crucial—unlike Siri and other mobile-app speech apps, (2) the interface enabled far-field interactions, meaning the user did not need to place the device near their mouth as they had to with the plain old telephone or with the smartphone and dictation microphones. (3) Most crucially, the user could engage with it while both their eyes and their hands were busy: they didn't need to look at anything, touch anything, or hold anything to interact with the speech system.

We, the authors of this book, are very much of that generation: we did enthusiastically believe in those early years that speech was around the corner; we were disappointed with every passing year that it had not arrived, but we kept our hope and our resolve alive, and now we do believe that speech has arrived. Also, because we are of that generation, we are averse to hype, and our critical, if not skeptical, eyes remain wide open.

A bit about this book.

This book focuses on a very specific type of interface: the voice first interface—or "voicebot" for short from now on. This is the interface that helps users with interactions where their eyes and their hands are not at their disposal—or where the users elect to not have them at their disposal: the users are under the hood of the car fixing an oil leak, potting a plant, taking a shower, lying in bed (half asleep), preparing food, in their car, blind or temporarily lost their sight, folding clothes and watching TV, tidying up the house, walking the dog, having a face-to-face conversation with someone, on a virtual call, typing away on their laptop, pecking at their smartphone, or in a museum staring at a painting. It is the challenge of designing for those myriad types of use cases that this book is for.

Therefore, this book does not touch on designing for nonvoice, text-based chatbots. Nor does it propose to help designers build multimodal interfaces. Designing multimodal interfaces, even those where voice is a central modality and the other modalities (screen, touch, haptic) play a supporting role, is an entirely different endeavor. Often, novice designers make the mistake of thinking of voice-centric multimodality as something like "voice first plus," when in reality it is its very own, separate type of interface, as different from voice first as it is from visual multimodality, where the visual modality and not the voice is at the center of the interface (for instance, the smartphone or the smart tablet).

A few words on the format. You will notice that this book does not make use of any visuals except at the very end, in our appendices. Our stand is this: if we are going to help the reader design compelling, effective, and even enjoyable voicebots, with the only tool at the disposal of both the designer and the user being spoken language and audio, we, the authors, had better be able to communicate our concepts and recommendations through pure language. This will hopefully illustrate how effective voicebot design can be delivered through the way we write and how we lay out our material.

You will also notice that we are short on wordy introductions, we avoid elaborations, and we usually skip neatly wrapping up chapters with conclusions. This is by design. If we are going to preach brevity, precision, and moving the conversation along as core principles of effective voicebot design, we had better reflect that in our writing style.

Speaking of style, this book is written in the spirit of the classic, English writing style guide, *The Elements of Style* by Strunk and White, a book that is familiar at least with most, if not all, English majors, and in fact probably anyone who took an English composition class. What makes that century-old tiny monograph, first published by Harcourt in 1920, a compelling book that has served generations of writers is its focus on the "bottom line." It is a book that cuts to the chase. Our aim is to emulate that style.

In addition, *The Elements of Style* was not meant to be the end-all text and final word about the topic of writing and composition but rather a handy manual for writers to use when they need actionable answers to concrete questions. This book is similarly meant to be used as a companion to, and not as a replacement for, all the excellent books on conversational voice design readily available to the designer. We provide a list of such books in our references section.

Who Should Read This Book?

The target readers of this book are budding and practicing voicebot designers in the newly emerging technology space of far-field voice, as delivered by platforms such as Amazon Echo and Google Assistant, and hearable/speakable technologies, such as Apple's AirPods. The book can also be useful for those who design IVR systems, but only to the extent that those systems are used eyes-free and hands-free.

While this book is meant primarily to help voicebot designers think through and make sound design decisions, we have written the book explicitly to be highly readable and jargon-free so that it is also accessible to those colleagues who work with a designer: user experience (UX) researchers, product managers, developers, testers, marketers, and business development professionals.

Why We Wrote This Book

This book aims to provide direct answers to questions such as "How do I design an effective opening interaction with a voicebot?" or "What should I keep in mind as I design for failures?" or "What are some best practices for designing a conversational voice help system?" Answers to such questions can sometimes be found in other books, but the reader usually has to look hard for them, and that person may need to look up several books before they find the answers. This book pulls together all such answers into one text and focuses on answering those questions directly and succinctly.

However, this book does not pretend by any means to provide final, immovable, timelessly frozen answers. Our aim instead is to crystalize the crucial questions the designer should ask themselves when they undertake the work; and then provide our answers, drawing on our decades-long experience designing and deploying voicebots. For instance, the designer needs to carefully consider how a conversation opens and that the first few seconds of an interaction are crucial and can spell the success or failure of the interaction. Someone who has never designed a voicebot before may not even be aware of how crucial those opening moments are. It may also not occur to that designer that the first-time user and the frequent user must be engaged differently, or that prompts should be crafted in such a way that the user knows what to say when the prompt completes, or that there are time-proven techniques for writing effective failure-recovery prompts. Teaching the designer how to critically grapple with the many challenges that they will face when designing voicebots is our main goal, not prescribing fixed and nonnegotiable recipes.

This book has a second, and perhaps more ambitious aim, which is to argue, and advocate through its recommendations, for the following: the practice of designing effective voicebots needs to free itself from the notion that the closer a voicebot mimics a human (for instance, through the sound of the voicebot's voice, the language it uses, the "persona" it assumes), the better will be the experience of the voicebot user. We believe this position—making a voicebot sound as human as possible—is as faulty as, say, stating that the way an adult speaks to a baby, or a child speaks to a dog, or a person speaks to someone who doesn't speak their language, are imperfect styles that should be improved upon and should emulate two humans fully competent in the language they are using while speaking with each other. We will advocate for the outlines of a style of interacting with voicebots that will borrow many of the ways humans speak to each other, but we will deviate, and at times in significant ways, from human-to-human speak.

Navigating This Book

The book is structured as follows:

- Introduction through Chapter 9 introduce the reader to foundational concepts about voice, audio, and conversation voice modeling.

- Chapters 10 through 19 focus on specific recommendations for specific challenges; for instance, what are effective ways to open a voicebot-to-human conversation? What techniques can the designer use to deliver clear, actionable prompts? How about when things go sideways? What techniques can the designer use to bring the interaction back on track?

- Last, Appendices A through C provide conceptual and practical tools that will help the designer effectively dissect their design strategy and sharpen their thinking approach.

By the end of this book the reader will be able to understand:

- How to craft just the right language to enable the voicebot to effectively communicate with humans.
- How to craft voicebots that are robust to failures.
- That voicebots are not humans and should always be designed with that basic fact in mind.
- That designing highly usable voicebots requires paying attention to a lot of "small details" that can make or break the experience.
- That while we, humans, are all competent conversationalists, we are by no means necessarily competent designers of voicebots. Designing compelling and effective voicebots is a lot of hard work and requires skills and intuitions that will only be built through years of direct, in-the-trenches practice.

O'Reilly Online Learning

 For more than 40 years, *O'Reilly Media* has provided technology and business training, knowledge, and insight to help companies succeed.

Our unique network of experts and innovators share their knowledge and expertise through books, articles, and our online learning platform. O'Reilly's online learning platform gives you on-demand access to live training courses, in-depth learning paths, interactive coding environments, and a vast collection of text and video from O'Reilly and 200+ other publishers. For more information, visit *https://oreilly.com*.

How to Contact Us

Please address comments and questions concerning this book to the publisher:

> O'Reilly Media, Inc.
> 1005 Gravenstein Highway North
> Sebastopol, CA 95472
> 800-998-9938 (in the United States or Canada)
> 707-829-0515 (international or local)
> 707-829-0104 (fax)

We have a web page for this book, where we list errata, examples, and any additional information. You can access this page at *https://oreil.ly/voice-first-style*.

Email *bookquestions@oreilly.com* to comment or ask technical questions about this book.

For news and information about our books and courses, visit *https://oreilly.com*.

Find us on LinkedIn: *https://linkedin.com/company/oreilly-media*.

Follow us on Twitter: *https://twitter.com/oreillymedia*.

Watch us on YouTube: *https://youtube.com/oreillymedia*.

Acknowledgments

First, our gratitude goes to our reviewers for their thoughtful suggestions and thought-provoking feedback: Bruce Balentine, Dr. Corey Miller, Jared Strawderman, Jonathan Bloom, Julia Anderson, Karl Melder, Lisa Falkson, and Rajiv Bammi.

A note of special thanks goes to the O'Reilly Media team for their hard work and support. We would like to especially thank Amanda Quinn for being our initial advocate for the book, Jill Leonard for her patience, kindness, and expert guidance throughout the process, and Kate Galloway who saw us through the million things that need to be done to deliver a complete, final book. Needless to say, we would not have made it without them.

Among many of our fellow Voice First travelers who over the years provided us opportunities and inspirations, taught us more than a thing or two, and worked with us to tackle real challenges and solve tough problems, are: Aaron Wellman, Adam Cheyer, Alireza Kenarsari, Dr. Alex Johnston, Alexa Juliana Ard, Amy Stapleton, Prof. André Oosterlinck, Ariane Nabeth-Halber, Audrey Arbeeny, Benjamin Falvo, Ben McCulloch, Beth Holmes, Bill Scholz, Bradley Metrock, Bret Kinsella, Brian Garr, Brielle Nickoloff, Carl Grant, Dr. Catherine Breslin, Cathy Pearl, Dan Miller, Daniel Hill, David Cuddihy, Dr. David Day, Prof. David Ferro, David Rennyson, David Toliver , Dr. Deborah Dahl, Derek Botten, Diana Deibel, Prof. Dirk Van Compernolle, Emily Banzhaf, Dr. Evelyne Tzoukermann, Gildie Nazari, Giorgio Robino, Ha-Hoa Hamano, Hassan Sawaf, Heidi Culbertson, Ilana Meir, Ivan Young, Janice Mandel, Jeanna Isham, Jeff Adams, Dr. Jintao Jiang, John Keeling, John Kelvie, Jon Stine, Dr. Joan Palmiter Bajorek, Prof. Joseph C. Pitt, Jonathan Piro, Jungyoon Koh, Kane Simms, Karen Kaushansky, Leor Grebler, Lisa Brandt, Lowell Robinson, Loyd Ford, Mai Tran, Dr. Maria Aretoulaki, Prof. Marjukka Ollilainen, Matthew Cadman, Mehedi Hasan, Michael Greenberg, Michael Zirngibl, Michelle Levine, Nathalie Scott, Navya Nayaki Yelloji, Neha Javalagi, Nicholas Sawka, Nicolo Scolieri, Noelle Silver, Paolo Narciso, Pete Erickson, Peter Krogh, Phillip Hunter, Rebecca Evanhoe, Richard Scarbath, Richard Warzecha, Roger Kibbe, Prof. Roger K. Moore, Ron Jaworski, Russ Elovitz, Ryan Elza, Sam Aparicio, Sarah Andrew Wilson, Sezen Uysal, Shyamala Prayaga, Prof. Steve Fuller, Susan Hura, Tomasz Jadczyk, Ulie Xu, Vishal Chordia, William Meisel, and Prof. Yisong Dai.

Finally, a special note of appreciation to our many, many mentors, colleagues, partners and friends over the years at Amazon, Angel.com, Apple, Convergys, Genesys, Google, Microsoft, MicroStrategy, MITRE, Schneider Electric, and Unisys. It has been, and continues to be, a wild and fun ride on the Voice First front.

And last but not least, to our son, Faris, for building the Amazon Echo skills and the Google Assistant actions that we needed while validating our examples and concepts: Thank you. And thank you for being a good sport and humoring our endless human language technology dinner table conversations over all these years.

Introduction

Voice is our most primordial means of communication. When we make it out of our mother's womb, the first thing that we do is to blare out our arrival at the top of our lungs. Our loud cry—our very first public statement—is rich in meaning: it tells the world that we are out, that we have arrived, that we have made it and are healthy; and it reminds everyone within earshot that even though we have many years to go to learn how to speak properly, we *will* express ourselves forcefully and we *will* communicate our needs without hesitation. And we will be doing all of this with *our voice*.

From that day on, we will indeed rely on our voice to communicate not only our needs, but later, to express our pleasure, discomfort, boredom, and delight. By the age of 18 months, we are learning at the astonishing rate of 10 words/day—a rate that we maintain well into adolescence.[1] And once we have learned how to string sentences together, we will turn into a veritable verbal torrent-producing machine. The average number of words spoken by an adult per day is 16,000 (and by the way, the average is gender neutral: women and men, it turns

---

1 Clifford Nass, *Wired for Speech: How Voice Activates and Advances the Human-Computer Relationship* (MIT Press, 2007), 1.

out, speak an equal number of words).[2] Compare this 16,000 words/day to the average number of words typed by an adult per day. The average person types something around 30 words per minute.[3] If you are continuously typing, the most you will type is around 1,800 words/hour. If you are constantly typing for 8 hours, you will type something close to 15,000 words. Unless you are a full-time, very focused, and highly dedicated data entry professional, the figure of the average number of words typed by an adult per day is much less than that: it's between 3,000 to 4,000 words.

So, in essence, we produce four to five times more meaning by speaking than we do by typing or writing. (Typing and writing, by the way, includes texting and tweeting.)

How about reading text versus listening to spoken words?

No matter how strong a reader you may be, you will consume far more meaning by listening than by reading. Think about all the meetings you participate in on a daily basis: the teleconference calls; the podcasts you listen to; the social audio sessions you attend; the casual chats you have, whether face-to-face or over the phone, with your family, colleagues, and friends; the lectures you attend; the radio you listen to; the videos you watch; and the TV shows you binge on. Compare all that to how much text you read daily: SMS texts, tweets, emails, documents, articles, books. Unless you are a graduate student cooped up in the library all day, the text you read doesn't even come close to the audio you passively and effortlessly hear.

So, in terms of pure volume, the bottom line is that we deliver and process far more meaning through audio than we do

---

2 Matthias R. Mehl et al., "Are Women Really More Talkative Than Men?" *Science* 317, no. 5834 (July 2007): 82.

3 C. Marlin Brown, *Human-Computer Interface Design Guidelines* (Ablex, 1988).

through all of the other media—probably all the other media combined.

But as the rest of this book will show, we hope, voice and audio are becoming our most compelling means of communicating with other humans not only because it is the most natural one—the one that we started using from day one—but also because it is by far the one that is most suited to a way of life that is becoming increasingly action-heavy. We are constantly doing, and we are doing it while on the move, and, crucially, we are doing it not only in collaboration with other people but also in collaboration with machines that are finally in a position to help us. These machines are helping us not just with things that are hard to do physically but also with things that are hard to do intellectually and cognitively. We need information quickly, and we have machines that can help us obtain that information. What is the fastest way of getting hold of that information? In many cases, it is by speaking. Not by typing, swiping, tapping, or pinching, but just by speaking. And so, just as we invented chainsaws and drills to get done what used to take a lot of effort, a great deal of skill, and toil, we have invented information technology that enables us to create, store, and retrieve information in a way that does not take a lot of effort, a great deal of skill, and toil to do.

We have lived long enough and witnessed firsthand the rise of the internet and all that its emergence has created, to state with little hesitation the following: just as we had no idea in 1982 what the world would look like in 2002, and just as we had no idea in 2002 what the world would look like in the year 2022, we believe that it is impossible to have any accurate ideas about what the world will look like in 2042. What we also do know is this: the best way to navigate the coming decades is to stick to some basic principles. We share five of them here.

First, we need, from the outset, to avoid the sin of establishing taboos and erecting dogmas. Yes, we need to establish rules, best practices, standards, and guidelines, and this book, for instance, is an exercise in exactly that. But whatever we propose, invent, agree on, and adopt, all of it must always be up for challenge. This ethos of constant revision is crucial given the basic fact that innovation is accelerating; hence, the need to quickly adapt to change is crucially compelling if we wish to take full advantage of the innovations we are creating.

Second, now that we can, we need to dive deep into whatever we are doing. *Excellence is rare because delivering excellence is very hard.* But excellence can become less rare if we adopt the ethos of diving deep into whatever we are doing. With tools, ecosystems, open source code, communities, growing, and thriving, we find ourselves increasingly in the exciting position of being able to focus on delivering on our ideas without having to waste enormous, precious resources on the means to enable those ideas. I don't have to buy an expensive server, install expensive software, or hire expensive people to launch a solid piece of technology. Cloud services with the software I need are available and affordable. So is affordable talent: the gig economy is here to enable me to engage with software developers from around the world. The result: My team and I can focus our time, energy, and money on diving deep into use cases and focusing on delivering true value that is easy to consume by my customers.

Third, we need to realize that with voice first, we are experiencing a major technological disruption of the same magnitude as the ones we saw with the introduction of the personal computer in the 1980s, the internet in the 1990s, the rise of the smartphone in the 2000s, and the use of social media in the 2010s. The 2020s are going to be the decade of voice first (among other things) and, in general, the decade where the ability to engage our world (physical and virtual) with both our eyes and hands no longer tethered to screens, big and small, is taken for granted. How is this realization useful? Mainly, it should at the very least prime us to think in deep and broad outlines and avoid comfortable parochial stances. For instance, when we start innovating in voice first, let's not spend our precious time and money on "voice enabling" what we can already do well with screens. Let's dig deep, understand what makes voice so different and special from the visual/tactile interface, and then build tools—in our case, voicebots—to deliver experiences that simply cannot be delivered with the screen-based interface. This book is all about getting the reader to be ambitious in that way: what voicebot can I build, and how well can I build it, so that my voicebot enables humans to do things they couldn't do before, or do but less clumsily, with less toil, less discomfort, and much greater ease than with anything other than my voicebot?

Fourth, within this ethos of diving deep, we need to make sure that we take seriously the one thing at the heart of what will enable us to deliver excellence, and that is: *taking context seriously*. And when we say context, we don't mean only the context of the person using our voicebot, but all contexts at all levels in the process of ideating, researching, building, and pushing voicebots to the real world. Then, crucially, keeping these voicebots alive and working hard in order to remain as useful as they can be for real people confronting real problems. Yes, we need to do our homework to understand the context of the use of the voicebot, but we must also understand that a successful voicebot will not survive in the real world unless we, its creators, take seriously *the context of its existence*. We have built a robust voicebot—good. But have we made our staff aware of its existence? Does the customer care team know about what the voicebot does and how it can help customers? Has this team invested any resources in communicating to the customers who can benefit from it? In the crushing majority of voicebot deployments today—very expensive deployments— the astonishing answer is no. Context at every single step is either ignored, touched on faintly, or touched on in a sloppy way. We have a long way to go on this score.

Last, let us always do what we can to build the right thing. In our context of voicebot building, let us make sure that we are *not* embracing foundationally dubious propositions, such as building voicebots that emulate human behavior. As we have already mentioned, and will repeatedly state in this book, a human being does not interact with voicebots the way they interact with other human beings. This may seem anodyne enough—and in fact it should be—but we have seen many instances where the designer is trying earnestly to make the voicebot act "naturally"—that is, sound and behave like a human being. But that is not the task of a voicebot designer. Their task is much simpler than that, and much more likely to deliver value, and even delight. A voicebot is a tool—a *mere tool*—that makes use of voice and sound to help a human being do something. The voicebot designer should always approach their work with an open, creative mind rather than artificially hem themselves into the corner of human emulation. We hope this book will help the reader take one step toward embracing that professional disposition.

CHAPTER 1

Why Voice First

Notwithstanding the massive adoption of laptops and smartphones, and the ubiquity of screens—whether gargantuan billboards or tiny ones on smartwatches—voice remains by far the medium that humans use the most to communicate with one another. We speak far more often than we type or touch. This even applies to a typical member of the Digital Generation. Watch gamers and note how much they verbalize their thoughts and feelings as they play; and note that those who watch them attend the sessions to listen to them talk as well as watch them play.

There are several reasons why voice is the predominant mode of communication. Here's a list of the key ones.

Eyes-Free

Unlike reading, listening does not require your eyes to be focused on anything to receive the information. We can have a conversation with our eyes closed. This opens up a world of possibilities. Communications can take place while doing any of the following: being in dark rooms; driving; watching TV; reading; taking a walk with someone else; potting a plant; admiring a landscape, typing; lying on the grass with hands crossed behind your head, side-by-side with a dear friend, staring at the sky; and so on.

Hands-Free

Similarly, unlike writing or typing, speaking does not require us to use our hands. We can hold a conversation with our hands occupied doing something: holding a book, typing on a laptop, preparing food, folding laundry, potting flowers, putting on our shoes, combing our hair, cutting coupons, putting on mittens, washing our hands, taking a bath or a shower, and so on.

Ephemerality

Unlike things that we type or images that we look at, a pure voice communication comes and goes, leaving no trace and nothing to clean up after the interaction is done. There are times when that is a limitation (think about the process of booking a flight or renting a car using the voicebot), but at other times, such ephemerality is a good thing: I get a piece of information, I respond, the thing gets it done, and I am back to my life stream; no text boxes or notifications to clear out, no browser tabs to kill.

Wealth

It is often said that a picture is worth a thousand words. But how many words—or even pictures—are worth a voiced, spoken word?

Take this sentence: "That's great—that's all we need!"

Let's say that that sentence was my friend's email response to a longer email I had sent them. Would you be able to tell me the meaning of that utterance just by looking at the text? Probably not. It could mean, "That's great! This is good news. Now, let's make the most of it," in response to my note: "We just got $500k in Angel funding!" Or it could be ironic: "That's great!— that's all we needed, wasting another daylong meeting talking nonsense" in response to my email, "Looks like George wants to do another daylong offsite."

Now imagine *hearing* the response: "That's great—that's all we need!" Chances are that you would probably be able to tell me, with minimal prior insight into the original email that I had sent, what the meaning of the response is: was it an expression of delight and an enthusiastic call to action, or bitter sarcasm?

In addition, you would probably be able to tell me whether the speaker is a man or a woman and, if the speaker is a mutual friend, you would be able to immediately identify them.

In general, a piece of audio is far more than simply spoken text. It can also communicate:

- Gender
- Identity
- Age
- Personality
- Mood/emotion
- Emphasis
- Ethnicity/region (through accent)

Passivity

Whereas we make an effort to read (at the very least, we physically hold a book or an eReader and need to stare at the words to read them), in the case of voice, the processing of the information is less demanding. We can lie down, close our eyes, and just listen to people talk.

Minimal Effort

In normal circumstances, uttering a few words to a smart speaker or to your AirPods is far less expensive for the user than typing text or navigating (tapping or swiping) on a small screen. No laptops or smartphones that need to be found, powered up, turned on, and signed into. If you can speak, you just speak.

Broadcasting

Unless I am writing on a whiteboard for an audience that is looking at my whiteboard, my writing is usually private or directed at a specific set of recipients. For instance, I send a written email to a specific set of coworkers, or I text with some specifically selected persons. In the case of speech, unless I consciously take precautions to limit my audience (close the door, speak softly), my spoken words are broadcast through physical space to whoever is within earshot. Often, this presents an issue: privacy. But at other times, the broadcast character of voice is an asset. For instance, let's say I have a smartphone application that tells jokes. In a setting where I have friends around me, sharing that joke by passing my smartphone around is not as compelling as having that joke voiced to everyone at the same time through my smart speaker.

Nonliteracy

With the spoken word, you don't need to know how to read or write in order to communicate. Think of the toddler being able to express their feelings, needs, and wants. Think also of the adult who is not literate enough to comfortably read or write. Unlike all other forms, voice does not expect you to have been trained in any special language, other than your mother tongue.

CHAPTER 2

When Voice First

Clearly, then, voice is no poor sibling of the other user interfaces: it stands on its own merits and has an important role to play in mediating interactions with our world, whether with other humans or with an artificial intelligence. But like all other interfaces, it is appropriate in certain contexts and it is not in others.

The four dimensions that need to be considered when assessing the suitability of a conversational voice first interface are environment, content, user state, and channels.

Environment

The first component of any context is the *environment surrounding the interaction*. Two types of environment are important for our purposes: *physical* and *social*:

Physical
> Characteristics of the physical environment that would be relevant to determining if voice is a good way to interact with the user is level of noise: if it's too noisy, don't use voice (because the user won't be able to hear the system and vice versa).

Social

> On the social dimension, if the user is in the company of other people, voice might not be the best way to interact (others may overhear the voicebot or the user; others may be bothered by the noise, etc.).

Content

Here, the concern is with three things: *what*, *how much*, and *persistence*. Following are descriptions of these content aspects:

What is being communicated?

- Sensitivity: If, for example, the information that needs to be communicated by the voicebot to the user is sensitive (date of birth, test results, bank account balance), then—unless no one is around and can overhear the interaction (remember, voice is usually public)—voice probably will not be the appropriate means of soliciting or delivering that information.

- Informational versus affective content: Am I going to share information with you (say, the business terms of a contract we are negotiating with a potential customer) or do I just want to catch up and shoot the breeze?

How much is being communicated?

> In human-to-human exchanges, if I want to send you a quick piece of information (e.g., my address), the best thing to do is to text it to you. If I want to engage with you about how best to strategize for a sales meeting, a phone call would probably be the right thing to do. In contrast, in human-to-voicebot interactions, the equation is flipped: humans don't want to hear voicebots speak for too long. If the voicebot has a quick tidbit of information (e.g., the store hours), then the voicebot should simply speak it. But if a lot of information needs to be communicated to a human, that information should be delivered to the

human in some other way: for instance, an email or a link to a page that has the information.

Persistence

Do we want to maintain traces of the communication once the communication has been carried out? I think it would be better for me to text you my address rather than call you and speak that address to you, that way you can have a record of it on your smartphone and maybe even click on it and have your smartphone's navigation provide you with routing directions. By the same token, if I don't want any trace of my communication with you, my best bet is to call you and privately speak with you. The same considerations should be looked at when designing a voicebot interaction.

User State

Here, the concern is with the properties of the human user as they engage with the voicebot.

Physical State

Is the user physically able to speak and listen? Are they hard of hearing? Do they speak slowly? Do they speak with a stutter?

Competency

Is the human who is interacting with the voicebot linguistically competent? That is, can they speak the language easily and comprehend it easily? For instance, if the voicebot is interacting with speakers who are just starting to learn English, then the voicebot should avoid using jargon. It should also speak more slowly and enunciate its words.

Availability

How much time does the user have available to engage with the voicebot? If we know that most of the users who will be interacting with the voicebot will be in a hurry when they engage with it, then openings should be quick, prompts need to be short, and the pace should be brisk. If someone is engaging a voicebot to help them pay for a parking spot, and they are engaging with it in the middle of a weekday, chances are that the user is pressed for time: they want to secure their spot quickly and move on.

Willingness

Is the human being known to refuse engaging with voicebots? Have they requested a human in the past at the very start of their engagement with voicebots, and done so consistently? If so, then the voicebot should not waste time: it should route them to a human agent or place them in the waiting queue.

Channels

To determine what is the best way to engage with a user, one needs to consider what channels they are likely to have at their disposal. Do they have access to a smart speaker, a smartphone, a landline, texting, email, chat, voicemail, video call? When you do your research, make sure you collect as much information as possible about what channels users will have access to. Your voicebot, no matter how well designed, will not be effective if you make wrong assumptions about how the voicebot can interact with the user. For instance, is the option of receiving a text of the address a viable option for most users of the voicebot?

Some Scenarios

Let's run through three scenarios to evaluate the suitability of voice interfaces given the above dimensions.

Scenario 1

A young woman who is driving a car to work wishes to hear a readout of her day's schedule. She is by herself:

- Environment: *Quiet* (if the windows are rolled down and the music is muted) and *private*.

- Content: Because the car is private and no one is in the car with her, the nature of content is not a factor. Also, the content is probably short (unless she has a very long day ahead of her).

- User state: Her hearing is normal and she wants to hear the schedule read out to her. Both her eyes (looking at the road) and her hands (on the steering wheel) are busy.

- Channels: She has car speakers that she is using and to which the voicebot is connected (think of an application like Siri).

In this case, the environment, content, user's state and channel fit very well together and will deliver a good experience to the user.

Scenario 2

A middle-aged woman who has just undergone a series of allergy tests wishes to get her results. She is at work in her cubicle. The results can be obtained by calling into a voicebot:

- Environment: *Quiet* but *not private*. Neighboring coworkers can hear the woman speak her patient ID number. A good designer, knowing if a user is calling the voicebot from a phone, would enable the user to enter their patient ID number by pressing the keypad.

- Content: The content spoken by the user is sensitive (her patient ID number, for instance). The content spoken by the voicebot is also sensitive (her medical information).

- User state: She has good hearing and has experience using the voicebot. Neither her hands nor her eyes are busy.

- Channels: The medium here is the telephone.

In this case, the voicebot could be ideal if the interface enabled the user to enter their patient ID using the keypad. Otherwise, the user would need to speak her ID number quietly enough not to be overheard, but not too quietly to challenge the voicebot's ability to recognize the patient ID. Perhaps a conversational text bot would be better, since the whole interaction would be through text, and moreover, the user would have the test results persisting (with perhaps a link to more information). But then again, the user may not want to have the test results persist (and would need therefore to delete the incoming text).

Scenario 3

I have signed up to be alerted when the plane of a friend I am picking up at the airport lands. I am at the airport, in a bar with a couple of friends, watching a baseball game:

- Environment: *Noisy*.

- Content: The content is something along the lines of: "Flight ABC has arrived at Gate XYZ." It is short and it is not sensitive.

- User state: I am having fun with my friends, watching the game.

- Channels: The smartphone.

In this case, the obvious best way to deliver the information is through a text message: the environment is too noisy, the content to be delivered is short, and I need it to persist. I don't want to have my fun interrupted by a phone call (it rings, I have to pick up, and I have to strain myself to listen).

CHAPTER 3

Why Voice First Automation

Let's take a step back and ask ourselves these basic questions: Why automate conversations in the first place? Why create voicebots? We laid out the case why we believe voice is a compelling medium and why a substantial portion of human-to-human communication is carried out through the medium of voice. But why create voicebots? What purpose do they serve?

One can create a voicebot for the sheer delight of creating something that attempts to emulate a human being in an activity that is quintessentially human. Or one can attempt to create a human-like sounding, human-like acting voicebot as a way to better understand the mechanics of human-to-human communication (say, in a research setting where such activities can help sharpen concepts, expose assumptions, put the spotlight on hidden biases).

In the world of business, the reasons for creating voicebots are concrete and straightforward. Here are some of them.

Reduce Costs

Like in the case of all automation, the voicebot is introduced to reduce cost in the quest to scale profitable growth. Specifically, in the business setting, the aim is to reduce the number of human agents needed to handle customer support cases. Why? Because a human agent's hour costs several dollars, while the voicebot's costs several cents.

Handle Spikes

Voicebots are also used to handle those periods when a contact center is flooded with emails, texts, and phone calls. A contact center may operate comfortably with 100 agents at normal volume levels, but during spikes, to offer approximately the same level of service to customers, the center may need to double the agent pool. Hiring 200 agents only to have 100 of them sit idly most of the time is an economically prohibitive proposition. The alternative is to make customers wait a lot longer than usual, which will result in customer dissatisfaction and trigger defection of existing customers to the competition—if the customer is opening tickets often and waiting long for the resolution of those tickets; or an outcome that is equally bad, a loss of a potential customer. Consider the following example: You are advertising your product on television; people love the product and so they call, only to be kept waiting for a long time before they get to speak to someone. A voicebot that can offload some of the traffic and successfully enable customers to self-serve would be an attractive option, but only as long as the *voice user interface* (VUI) is designed and implemented with the goal of empowering the user to complete their tasks rather than, say, simply occupying them with entering information that may or may not be used by the human agent when the customer is connected to them.

Increase Customer Satisfaction

Customer satisfaction can be accomplished in several ways:

- Empowering the customer to serve themselves. This is usually most effective when the tasks are simple (looking up order status, making a payment, finding out what the store hours are) or when the customer is very familiar with the VUI.

- Shortening the customer's wait time. Even when a given customer opts not to use the voicebot, the fact that others are using it (i.e., self-serving) shortens the length of the wait queue and therefore the length of the wait time.

- Enabling the customer to serve themselves after hours, when the contact center is closed and no agent is available to handle the customer.

- Giving the customer a choice. People don't like being forced to follow one path or another. They don't like it when they are forced to serve themselves and they don't like it when they are forced to wait (and in some cases, they do not want to speak to a human when what they want to do is very simple: for instance, find out what the store hours are). By giving the customer a choice, those customers who decide to engage the voicebot have self-selected: they are those who are most predisposed to be cooperative with the voicebot and hence the ones with the greater likelihood of successfully engaging the voicebot.[1]

Increase Agent Satisfaction

By enabling customers to engage voicebots to handle simple requests, you are by definition reserving agents to tackle those customer requests that are more challenging and require the intelligence, sophistication, and knowledge of the human agent. Professional support agents are in the service business: they want to serve customers and help them solve problems. And the more challenging the problem, the more the professional

---

1 See Stephanie Staton, "Vodafone Spain Drives Customer Satisfaction with Speech," *Speech Technology Magazine* (March 1, 2007). *http://www.speechtechmag.com/Articles/Editorial/Deployments/Vodafone-Spain-Drives-Customer-Satisfaction-with-Speech-29711.aspx.*

agent will use their intelligence, sophistication, and knowledge, so that when the problem is solved, the human agent will feel good about themselves: they get to be that professional version of themselves they are proud of. Compare how such a human agent feels at the end of a day to that agent who handled an endless stream of requests that could be easily handled by anyone (store hours, addresses, when the power will be back on, etc.).

Increase Revenue

In those instances where you have a product or a service that can be easily ordered or an upgrade that can be easily selected, a well-designed voicebot can help you ensure that you are able to empower buyers to buy at any time during the day and not just when human agents are available.

Moreover, a voicebot that is designed carefully and well would be able not only to sell but also to up-sell or cross-sell the right products and services to the right people, and, crucially, do so consistently and systematically. Unlike your pool of human agents, some of whom may be trained better than others, and some of whom may be having a bad day and not able to bring their A game, your voicebot is the same for every customer and will always bring their same game (an A game if well designed, an otherwise game if otherwise).

Enable Personalization

Computers are very good at systematically executing complex algorithms, using reams of data, and then delivering the results at the speed of light. A human agent can at best deliver results at the speed of a phone call, in some instances requiring, for example, time pauses to look up information or consult with someone else who has the knowledge. More daunting than fetching information that someone has is inferring what a customer is calling about, for instance. The human agent may need to factor in the customer's area code, the time of day and day of week they are calling, what were the last interactions they engaged in (bought a product, checked the status of an order, etc.), what other people are calling other agents about; and then from all that data, infer what they may be calling about. Perhaps they are calling about a product that was just introduced, or about an outage, or about the delivery that is 2 days overdue and about which they have called 3 times in the last 24 hours. More complex still may be determining what product or service to mention to them as a possible up-sell or cross-sell opportunity. All of the above, if the right system and VUI are designed, can be easily and systematically delivered by a voicebot, and nearly impossible by a human agent.

Facilitate Task Completion

Often, what bewilders voicebot users are the confusing options they need to pick from in order to execute a task. By its very nature, a VUI is a constraining medium. And as we have seen, this creates a challenge for the designer to put together a usable VUI. At the same time, such constraints can be used to advantage. VUI interactions are linear and, in many situations, that is precisely what is called for: an assistant that handholds the customer and guides them through the process one step at a time to complete a transaction.

Secure Privacy

An impersonal voicebot is sometimes exactly what the customer wants if the interaction they are about to engage in is private or embarrassing: e.g., finding out medical test results for certain types of illnesses, paying a fine, or finding out what their low bank balance is.

Increase Security

Interactions where sensitive information is being exchanged (credit card information, account numbers, PINs) are ideally suited for voicebot. Two types of concerns are effectively addressed:

- Giving sensitive information to a human agent and risking the agent misusing that information (e.g., credit card numbers).

- Having someone fake one's identity (someone acquiring one's account and PIN information and calling in to execute a transaction over the phone). In this latter case, voice biometrics technology can effectively neutralize this risk by having the voicebot analyze the customer's voice to determine if their identity claim is legitimate.

CHAPTER 4

The Three Core Characteristics of the VUI

Although automatic speech recognition has made significant strides in the last few years, it remains an imperfect technology that has earned the skepticism of human users. But what is truly at fault is not any technology in itself but the misuse of that technology. The voice user interface (VUI) is a powerful interface in well-defined circumstances and use cases. Deploy a VUI in the right conditions and you will have a truly delighted user. Attempt to use voice in the wrong conditions (e.g., the task is complex and requires referring to multiple pieces of information; noisy environment; the user is hard of hearing; the interface asks the user confusing, long-winded questions) and the result is at the very least an irritated user.

A common misconception the novice VUI designer often suffers from is the belief that designing a VUI consists of taking a graphical user interface (GUI) and "simplifying it" and then giving it a voice. After all, while only a very small minority of people can claim some visual talent (e.g., drawing), the vast majority of us can safely claim to be expert conversationalists— or at least competent enough to design a simple interaction between a human being and a computer. So, often, especially in situations where a successful visual/tactile interface has already been deployed, a big mistake is made: the people who designed the GUI are tasked with delivering a "voice version" of that experience.

As we will argue in later chapters, the key to delivering a successful experience is the extent to which the use case and the interface fit with each other (i.e., the interface delivers an experience that solves the use case). If you have a fit, the user will be delighted. If you have a misfit, the user will abandon the interface or will use it unhappily.

The designer of a VUI must keep the following three core aspects of conversational voice in mind.

Time Linearity

Unlike graphical interfaces, voice interfaces are linearly coupled with time. When you are reading text on a web page, for instance, you can easily skip ahead with your eyes to the section you are interested in. Not so with a voice interface, where you must patiently listen to one word before you can hear the one that follows it. Here are examples of concrete guidelines that flow directly from this basic fact:

Avoid long prompts
> Obviously, unnecessarily long prompts will quickly tax the user's patience. Long prompts explaining how the voicebot works, for instance, may be inevitable and necessary with a novice user, but they should not be forced upon an expert user. So, try to differentiate at the outset between novice and expert users, and use short, to-the-point prompts with the experts and longer ones with novice users.

Use short menus
> The length of an alphabetically sorted drop-down menu on a web page is a nonissue. The length of a menu in a voice interface, on the other hand, should not exceed five or six.

Put important information first
> Don't annoy the user by having them listen to unnecessary noise for the information they need. Give them what they want up front.

Allow interruptions
> The ability to interrupt is usually a must-have when dealing with nonnovice users. People who know what they want to do, what to say, and how to say it, don't want to wait for the voicebot to finish talking before they can give their response.

Offer shortcuts for the user who knows what to do
> Another must for nonnovice users are shortcuts that cut through menus and get the user to what they want to do or where they want to be in a dialog.

Allow pauses
> An enormous advantage that a graphical interface has over a voice interface is the ability of the user to easily pause and pick up where they left off. We do this without even thinking when we read a piece of text. During voice interactions where the user may need to pause and do something, make sure you offer that option. For instance, if the user needs to take down a long series of numbers (say a confirmation code), ask them to go ahead and get paper and pencil and to say, "Continue," when they are ready.

Unidirectionality

Compounding the linearity of speech is its unidirectional character. Just as time is a one-way street, speech is a one-way medium. When you hear something, you can't easily go back and listen to it again. Contrast this to reading a piece of text where you can readily scan a couple of paragraphs, or even pages, then go back and reread the text. There are ways to handle this issue:

Offer to repeat

One obvious way to alleviate this limitation is to offer the user the ability to have information repeated to them. Of course, make sure the user is aware that they can have information repeated to them by informing them of this ability at the beginning of the interaction and any time where important information is given out to them.

Offer help

Crucial information such as instructions given at the start of the interaction should be available for the user to tap into at any point in the exchange. Offer instructions on how to access help at the beginning of the interaction and at moments where the user is at a loss over what to do (e.g., at no-input or a no-match).

Offer summaries

In interactions where information is being gathered from the user or given out to them in a stepwise fashion, a powerful technique to overcome the unidirectionality of voice interfaces is to offer users the ability to ask for a summary of information collected so far.

Invisibility

Perhaps the most frustrating thing about using a voice interface is the feeling of not knowing precisely *where* you are in the interaction and *what* exactly the assistant expects you to do next. A well-designed web site will *show* navigators where in the menu tree they are, but even without a menu path indicator, a web page usually has enough visual clues to tip the user on where they are in the site—a URL being one simple indicator. Not so with a voice interface, where the user can quickly feel lost for a lack of mental markers positioning them where they precisely are in the exchange with the assistant. There are ways to correct this:

Mark the exchange

Just like a well-designed web page will indicate where in the web site a user is, a good voice interface will tell the user where in the conversation they are positioned. Usually, a few will suffice: "Looking up transactions" before engaging in an exchange where the user wishes to find out their latest bank transactions, or "Quizzing" before beginning or resuming a quiz sequence.

Trace the path

In interactions where the conversation structure is deep and wide, users can very easily become confused about where they are in the interaction, even when you mark the individual levels. In such situations, you can associate with each dialogue state that handles an interaction a "position marker" that traces, starting from the main menu, the position of the user within the menu tree. The voicebot saying something as succinct as "Restaurants, Chinese, Zip code," for instance, could help the user understand that they chose "Restaurants," then "Chinese," and are now being asked, or were asked, for a zip code to locate Chinese restaurants within that zip code. The designer can be less succinct with alternative phrasing such as, "We are looking for Chinese restaurants and the next thing I need from you is your zip code." The main idea is to give a way for the user to situate themselves in a complex exchange with the voicebot.

Use earcons

An earcon, or auditory icon, is the voice equivalent of a graphical interface's icon. An icon is a small graphic that means something specific in the context of an interaction—for instance, an arrow pointing to the right may mean go to the next page, and one to the left may mean go back to the previous page. Earcons can be very useful in positioning the user within a conversation or in announcing the type of action that is about to be undertaken. For example, the sound of a keyboard clicking could be used to indicate to the user that the voicebot is busy doing something (while dead silence may be taken by the user that the assistant crashed or the call had ended).

Perhaps the one fundamental advantage that GUIs have over VUIs is the feeling that a graphical user has control over both the medium and the interaction. A bad GUI can certainly frustrate the user, but it does take a very bad GUI to throw the user into a state of utter confusion. A VUI, on the other hand, because it is time-linear, unidirectional, and invisible, has to stumble only a couple of times in the interaction for the user to be thrown into a state of confusion. Keeping in mind that there are key differences between designing a GUI and a VUI should help the alert VUI designer avoid making the costly mistake of smuggling GUI assumptions when engaged in VUI design.

CHAPTER 5

The Elements of Conversation

With one burst of energy, I can issue a pretty sophisticated directive, such as, "Get me one large turkey hoagie with everything on it, and a small Coke."

Think about how many steps it would take me to communicate that same command in a graphical user interface, say on an iPhone. I'd have to select the sandwich (turkey hoagie) from a drop-down list of sandwiches, then I would need to select the size of the sandwich (another drop-down maybe), then I would click on the "all" toppings checkbox (assuming this option was offered), and finally I would need to select the drink and its size. That would be at least five distinct steps (and this doesn't even include the tap(s) for unlocking the app). That's clearly far more effort than speaking one sentence. In the case of the one spoken sentence, the effort equation is shifted away from the user and onto the interface: the user can speak naturally (they don't need to use the artificial devices of drop-down menus, checkboxes, radio buttons, etc.) so that the burden is on the voicebot to figure out what the user wants by interpreting the words they speak.

The ability of a voicebot to parse a rich, complex user statement, however, does not obviate the need for the voicebot to engage the user in a stepwise, back-and-forth interaction. Users don't pack their commands to the hilt just to save steps. They will try to be efficient, but only to a point. When I call to order a pizza, I don't say in one breath, "I want two large pizzas, both thin crust; I want the first to have pepperoni, beef, and black olives, and on the second, I want chicken, green peppers, and extra tomatoes; for drinks, I also want two large bottles: one Coke and one Sprite." I have somehow come to learn that people can't take more than two or three pieces of information at a time, and so, instead, a more natural flow might be something along these lines:

> AGENT: Hello. Alphonso's Pizza. Can I take your order?
>
> ME: Yes. I want to order two large pizzas, please. Both thin crust.
>
> AGENT: OK. What would you like on your first pizza?
>
> ME: Pepperoni, beef, and black olives.
>
> AGENT: OK. That's pepperoni, beef, and black olives.
>
> ME: Yup. And the second pizza…
>
> AGENT: Yes.
>
> ME: I want chicken, green peppers, and extra tomatoes.
>
> AGENT: That's chicken, green peppers, and extra tomatoes, correct?
>
> ME: That's right.
>
> AGENT: Any drinks?
>
> ME: Yes. Two large bottles, one Coke and one Sprite.
>
> AGENT: Two bottles. Coke and Sprite. Anything else.
>
> ME: No, that's it.
>
> AGENT: Etc.

We are calling the mechanism that enables the methodical exchange of structured information a *conversation*, and we, humans, are masters in the art of conversing. Even the most involved of conversational exchanges come to us very naturally. And yet, upon closer observation, the simplest of conversations turns out to be an impressively complex endeavor. Conversations are not simply interactional dyads. They are highly structured and closely regulated interactions. Pulling off a successful conversation that accomplishes its goals requires close and careful management by all participants.

In this chapter, we describe the basic mechanism that is used by participants in a conversation to successfully start and complete conversations.

The four key concepts used to describe the conversational mechanism are: *action*, *state*, *context*, and *signaling*.

The Ontology of Conversations

In order to introduce the concepts of action, state, context, and signaling, the first step is to settle on an ontology—a way of slicing the world that gives "shape" to objects. Unless we have objects that have properties, we can't talk about actions, states, contexts, and signalings.

Let's start with the ontology of a conversation; that is, the main objects that make up the world of conversations.

Participant

This is a person or a voicebot that is engaged in a conversation. Participants are the primary actors: they start a conversation, stop it, pause it, end it; they provide its content and its tone; and they are the ones who manage it along the way.

Statement

This refers to what participants speak (or do not speak), including how the content is spoken: the words that are said (or not said), intonations used, pauses (or nonpauses when pauses were expected), omissions (or nonomissions), violations of maxims (or their observance), etc. For instance, not saying anything when the voicebot asks you a question is a statement, and it has meaning (for instance, "I didn't understand your question" or "I'm distracted" or "I didn't hear you because we have a spotty connection," etc.). This statement just happens to be a statement without words (just as zero is a number that denotes the absence of quantity).

Turn

This is the conversational "real estate" within which participants communicate their statements. Technically, a turn is an interval of time during which one of the participants has the floor, so to speak. It is important to note that a turn is not simply the period of time during which a person is speaking: a person may own a turn and yet no one is speaking (when, for instance, the conversation is paused because the owner of the turn needed to take another call); someone may be speaking out of turn under the protest of the turn owner, or may be speaking with the permission of the turn owner, but only for the duration of the permission, with the owner having the right to reclaim their turn at any time.

Conversation

The conversation is itself an object in the ontology. Conversations have properties: they are short, long, focused or all over the place; they have a starting point (once they come into existence) and an endpoint (once they have been ended). Conversations move from one state to another state: nonexistent to started, then progressing, then possibly paused, then ended.

Moreover, each of these four objects (participant, statement, turn, conversation) can itself be the topic of a conversational statement during a conversation. We can pause a conversation and later come back to it by saying, "So, where did we leave things last time?" Or during a conversation, one could refer to a statement that was spoken a couple of minutes ago. Or one may react to an interruption from you by saying, "Hang on, it's my turn to speak." Or one can even refer to the very conversation itself, as in, "I'm glad we are having this talk."

The Conversational Actions

As noted above, conversational actions are taken through *statements*, by *participants*, to take the *conversation* from one *state* to another. Here are the main actions:

Start conversation

> These are the actions taken by the initiator of the conversation, and in the context of human-to-human conversations, they usually consist of brief, formalized greetings, such as "Hello" or "Hi"; or, in the case of a voicebot, a wake word that the user speaks; or, if the voicebot is the one initiating the conversation, a sound or a chime that the user has come to know to mean that the voicebot wishes to engage in a conversation.

Articulate content

> This is the action of the human or the voicebot providing content. The content could be information, a question, some sound, or even silence.

Offer turn

> A turn is usually offered implicitly by the cessation of talking. If a participant stops talking, that in itself is usually (but not always) a signal that the counterpart should now assume the conversational turn. At times, a participant may explicitly offer the turn if they feel that their counterpart is not interpreting the silence as a turn offer ("Go ahead!") or is reluctant to take the turn ("Your turn; what do you think?")

Request turn

> In human-to-human conversations, a participant may request a turn by either silently signaling that they wish to speak (raising a finger, moving the head back, opening the mouth), or by barging in; they could do it gently, by clearing their throat, speaking a hesitant word,

politely requesting the turn ("May I interject?") or outright attempting to take the turn over by speaking over the turn owner. In the case of human-to-voicebot—at least in its current state of the art—humans simply seize the turn rather than request it.

Cede turn

This is the action of a turn owner ceding ownership of a turn upon request of the turn by the other participant. Note that ceding is not the same as offering: a participant cedes only if they believe their counterpart in the conversation is requesting the turn. Turn ceding may be accomplished silently (the owner ceases speaking) or explicitly ("Please, go ahead").

Retain turn

A turn owner, by virtue of being the owner (and being recognized as such by virtue of the turn being previously relinquished to them) has the privilege of retaining a turn that is being requested. The turn owner may decide to retain the turn by either explicitly rejecting the request to relinquish the turn ("Hang on, I'm not done") or implicitly rejecting that request (they continue talking and ignore the request).

Seize turn

A turn is seized when a participant who is not the current owner of the turn assumes ownership of the turn in spite of the current owner's attempt to retain it.

Interrupt

Participants often interrupt each other—sometimes to request the turn, while at other times, to simply to add something on the side without requesting the turn or fully taking it over.

Pause

Conversations are started and ended, but they are also paused. The pause may be explicit: a participant may say, "Hang on one sec—I need to take this"; or, perhaps when interacting with a voicebot, the user pushes a specific button to pause the exchange. The pause may be implicit: some external event interrupts the conversation—for instance, the boss pops her head in while you are chatting with your colleague and you and your colleague stop talking to each other and direct your attention to the boss.

Pausing in the context of a voicebot introduces some unique challenges. In the context of the traditional telephony-based voicebot, pausing is a somewhat unnatural action. A phone call is expected to be briskly moving along, inexorably, toward completion. Phone calls are time-boxed activities: they have a very well-defined start time (when the voicebot picks up), and an equally well-defined end time (the hang-up event). In the interim, the user is expected to fully dedicate their attention to the task at hand—their exchange with the voicebot—until the phone call is completed or the customer is routed to a human being. Compare this interaction with, say, an iPhone app. At any time, the user of an iPhone app can perform an action to minimize the app. What that action usually means is: (pause) I need to do something else and I want to pause my interaction with you. I may or may not come back, but that's something I will decide later. Meanwhile, remember where we were.

Resume after pause

Pause resumption introduces a host of interesting questions in the context of a voice conversation: Should the conversation pick up where it left off? Who owned the turn? How long ago was the conversation paused? Was it so long ago that the participants would need to be reminded where the conversation left off, or was it so recent (a few seconds ago) that it should pick up right where it left off? And was there information that was offered that is now no longer valid? Think of an exchange between you and a voicebot that was helping you book a hotel room. Say the conversation was paused several hours ago and that it was paused at the point where you were providing your payment information. How should the conversation resume? Obviously, at a minimum, a recap is in order, reminding the user of the information provided so far and where the conversation was paused. But a smart voicebot would first check to make sure that any information that was provided (for instance, availability of hotel room, room rates) has not changed since the interaction before recapping it.

Repeat

Conversational voice interactions are ephemeral. Unlike, say, texting or instant messaging (for example, Slack channel chat), a pure voice conversation leaves no visual traces to be consulted during or after the conversation. As a result, participants will need to ask their counterpart to repeat themselves. Repeats may be requested explicitly ("Can you repeat that, please?"), may be offered explicitly ("Do you want me to repeat that?"), or may be offered outright ("That's 77812. Repeat: 77812").

Start over

The drastic measure of restarting a conversation is rarely needed when both participants are human, but it is a useful method when a human is interacting with a voicebot and either the human participant or the voicebot decides that it is best to reset the conversation rather than repair it or pick up from where it left off.

Terminate

Conversations end in one of two ways: *cooperatively* (both participants agree to end the conversation) or *unilaterally* (with one participant ending the conversation without bothering to cooperate with their counterpart). Human conversations almost always end cooperatively, with the intentionally unilateral ending of a conversation carrying a strong connotation of conflict. Conversations between a human and a voicebot, on the other hand, are often ended unilaterally, usually by the human participant (e.g., having received the information about their date of the last payment received, the customer stops the exchange).

The Conversational States

In the context of a human interacting with a voicebot, the following states are identified:

Not started
> No conversation is taking place and, crucially, no conversation is in a paused state.

Speaking
> Either the human or the voicebot is speaking.

Listening
> Either the human or the voicebot is listening.

Paused
> The conversation is paused.

Processing/thinking
> Either the human or the voicebot is processing some input.

Ended
> The conversation that took place between a human and a voicebot has ended. It is important to note that a paused conversation is not the same as one that has ended.

The Internal Conversational Context

The internal conversational context is described by identifying the turn owner, the action being taken, the state of the participants, and the information collected so far. As we mentioned in the Introduction, we distinguish the *internal conversational context* from the *external conversational context*, which refers to the conditions within which the conversation is taking place—for instance, the physical context (a noisy environment), the emotional context (the human is in distress), and other such considerations.

As an example, in the pizza ordering example earlier in this chapter where I said, "Yes. Two large bottles, one Coke and one Sprite":

- Turn owner: Human
- Action: Providing content (saying "Yes")
- State: Talking
- Information: Pizza 1 (size = large, crust = thin, topping 1 = pepperoni, topping 2 = beef, topping 3 = black olives); Pizza 2 (size = large, crust = thin, topping 1 = chicken, topping 2 = green peppers, topping 3 = extra tomatoes)

Conversational Signaling

Crucial to managing conversations is the continual signaling by the participants to each other. In the context of interactions between humans and voicebots, two types of signaling are identified: (1) *signaling states* and (2) *signaling transitions* between states. In what follows, we describe the types of signaling that a voicebot needs to issue to the human to ensure that the human is aware of the voicebot's state.

Signaling States

Here are the five conversational states that the voicebot needs to signal to the human to ensure smooth conversational flow:

Initial/rest
    This signals that the voicebot is ready to engage.

Listening
    This is the crucial feedback provided to the user that the voicebot is actively listening. This often takes the form of visual fluttering or pulsing, indicating that the audio

stream issued by the human is being actively received by the voicebot.

Processing/thinking

This signaling occurs when the human has stopped speaking, but before the voicebot has responded verbally. This signaling is usually delivered with a sound, something along the lines of light percolation.

Speaking

This signaling occurs by virtue of the sound being made by the voicebot as it speaks its response.

Paused

This is the state that indicates that the voicebot was interrupted and is in a state of suspension. The difference between an initial state and a paused state is the absence of context in the former and the existence of one in the latter.

Signaling Transitions

Equally crucial to signaling states is signaling transitions between states. There are three signals a voicebot sends to a human user:

Started listening

This signal by the voicebot to the user shows that the voicebot has started listening and that they, the human user, now own the turn.

Finished listening

This is a signal by the voicebot to the user that the voicebot has stopped listening and that they, the automated voicebot, now own the turn.

Finished interacting

This is a signal by the voicebot to the user that the voicebot has stopped interacting with the user. This usually takes place when the human user says something like "Stop" or "I'm done" or does not respond to repeated requests for a response from the automated voicebot.

Equipped with an ontology (a slicing up of the world) and a collection of concepts, let's now take a look at the sequence of starting a voice-only phone conversation between two humans to illustrate how these convepts can help us break apart the elements of the conversation. In other words, let's see if the ontology and concepts that emerged from it can do some work for us:

- I pick up the phone, dial up my friend Jodi, listen to the phone ring a few times, and wait for her to pick the phone.

- After three rings, Jodi picks up the phone and says "Hello!" to which I respond, "Hey, Jodi!"

- In this sequence, we went from a state where no conversation existed to a state where a conversation has now been started.

- My action of picking up my phone, dialing Jodi's phone number, and letting her phone ring three times will mean to Jodi that I probably want to talk to her, unless it was an unintentional dial—for instance, I accidentally clicked on her phone number in an email that contained it.

- My friend's action of picking up the phone and saying "Hello" means to me that Jodi is available and ready to engage, and now would like me to respond to her "Hello."

- If she does not pick up the phone, it may mean, among other things, that she is busy and can't take my call, that the phone is not near her, or that she is just not in the mood to talk to me.

- If she does pick up and I respond with "Hey, Jodi," this means that I *did* mean to call her and that I would like to engage with her in a conversation.

- At which point, having heard me and wanting to engage, Jodi may respond with "Hey!," an action signaling that indeed a conversation has now been established and has been started, taking us now fully into the *conversation started* state.

Note how Jodi's initial action of saying "Hello!" is followed by another action: the action of not speaking—silence. The purpose of this second action is to hand over to me the conversational turn, which she owns immediately after she accepts the call. This is worth noting: if Jodi was not available to engage with me but wanted to be polite, she could have started the conversation with "Hello!" and immediately followed it with, "Can I call you back in like 10 minutes? I'm in the middle of another call."

My response of "Hey, Jodi" to Jodi's second action—silence—means that I have accepted her offer for me to take the turn and that I am willing to engage with her in a back and forth conversation.

Jodi's next response ("Hey there!") is in fact two actions packed into one utterance: by speaking, my friend acknowledges my greeting, but also agrees to take the turn back and to engage. "Hey there" means (at least in part): "I am available and ready to speak with you."

Depending on the tone, or some other indicators—such as the slightest pause or hesitation with which Jodi articulated her "Hey there"—she could come across as saying, "I am angry at you, but I am available and ready to speak with you," or "What a pleasant surprise! I am available and ready to speak with you," or "I'm feeling a bit down, but I am ready to speak with you," and many other variations, depending on our respective moods, our relationship, our respective contexts, and various other considerations.[1]

---

1 Elizabeth Stokoe, *Talk: The Science of Conversation* (London: Robinson, 2018).

In this chapter, our aim has been to describe the mechanism of conversation that is used by participants to engage each other in voice and audio interactions, and to delineate an ontology of the objects that populate the world of conversations. The four key concepts that we used to describe the mechanism are action, state, context, and signaling. The ontology we delineated consists of participants, statements, turns, and conversations. During a conversation, a participant takes an action within a turn and a context to bring about a state that is signaled by the participant through a statement.

With this conceptual framework at hand, we are now ready to begin laying down the foundation for the next level of concepts: the norms and rules that participants observe, ignore, or violate, to generate meaning as they engage each other in conversational interactions.

CHAPTER 6

The Rules of Conversation

Language is far more than a mere collection of symbols that human beings use to exchange information about themselves and the world around them. Words exist for acting upon the world,[1] and they are always used within a context: they are used by people (or by machines), at a certain time, at a certain place, with a set of goals or intentions to create some effect or counteraction, and they are directed to a certain audience. More than that, they are spoken or written within a stream of other words, and they are delivered in a certain way.

We saw in Chapter 1 the example of the meaning of "That's great!—that's all we need!" and how it varied depending on whether it was said in response to a statement that announced good news (the reaction expressing happiness and enthusiasm) or in response to a statement that announced not so good news (expressing deflation and dismay). In the context of active, real-time conversations between humans (for instance, telephone conversations), the context is immediate and the full meaning of words and statements is being constructed by a complex set of influences. How the conversation was started,

---

1 John Searle, *Speech Acts: An Essay in the Philosophy of Language* (Cambridge University Press, 1969).

for instance, immediately creates a context and framing that can greatly influence the rest of the exchange: was it opened with a perfunctory "Hello" or was the "Hello" skipped, with the person instead opening with, "What's going on here?" (signaling distress or anger) or "So, this is what I think…" (expressing intimacy and informality that would be marred with a perfunctory greeting). All along the conversation, the meaning of what is said will heavily depend on things like the volume used to speak a statement, its intonation and emphasis, whether it was said with hesitation or said firmly, whether it was followed by a chuckle or a yawn. In other words, the meaning of whatever is said is a creature of the precise flow between the conversational participants. Moreover, each participant will have their own interpretations of meaning, and the respective interpretations may at times widely diverge and vary one from the other: I may have spoken something in jest only to have it be interpreted literally, nonironically by my counterpart. And when I detect the misalignment, I will probably explicitly communicate to them my detection of the misalignment, as in, "Come on, you can't be serious. You know I was joking!"

At first glance, then, the complexity of conversations may leave us with the impression that conversational interactions are highly entropic activities and much too chaotic for systematic modeling. But in fact, it turns out that conversations are highly structured interactions and observe a well-defined set of rules. Adherence to these rules is expected, while deviations from them become a source of meaning. For instance, just like the volume with which a statement is spoken would be a source of meaning during a verbal exchange (e.g., someone raises their voice in anger), the act of someone suddenly changing topics on us during a conversation would also be a source of meaning that we would note and try to actively interpret and understand. But more than that, deviations from the official protocol can themselves be devices that the participants purposefully use to establish just the right protocol that best suits the conversational situation. For instance, two intimate friends conversing might skip formalities, interrupt each other, and finish each other's sentences when they are engaged with each other; in other words, engage in behavior that would be deemed inappropriate between two people who are not intimate with each other. Or those very two friends may revert to the formal protocol to signal that the situation is not normal; for instance, they are mad at each other or are in a social setting where such behavior is not appropriate.

Deviations from expected behavior can not only reflect relationships (e.g., friendship) and circumstances (a formal dinner party) but can themselves be transformational. A person wishing to get closer to another person may intentionally diverge from the protocol to signal their intention to become more intimate and effect that intimacy through that action if the other person accepts the divergence. For instance, instead of opening a conversation with a formal "Hello," the person wishing to move closer to the other person may open it with "So, I had this thought...." Should the other person accept this offer at establishing intimacy, then intimacy is established, while if the other person feels the attempt presumptuous, they could respond with, "Sorry, who is this?"

So, yes, conversations are bewildering in their complexity, and human beings are impressively effective at navigating such complexity, but conversations are certainly not chaotic. In fact, that complexity is made possible precisely because a well-defined, commonly adopted protocol is available to both participants who use that protocol (as well as acts of adherence and nonadherence to it) to send signals to each other at many levels.

A structuring paradigm that we have found useful in making sense of why people behave the way they do when they engage in conversations with each other is the one proposed by the British philosopher of language, Paul Herbert Grice.[2] Grice

---

2 Paul Grice, "Logic and Conversation," in *The Logic of Grammar*, ed. D. Davidson and G. Harman (Dickenson, 1975), 64–75.

stipulated that conversations are governed by a guiding principle and four maxims.[3] When humans enter into a conversation with each other, Grice proposed, this guiding principle and the four maxims come into play in ways that help the participants predict behavior and extract and create meaning.

The Cooperative Principle

Let's begin by taking a step back and defining what we mean here by *conversation*. For our purposes, a conversation is an exchange willingly entered between two participants for the purpose of accomplishing a specific goal or a set of goals. In other words, when two people enter into a conversation, they are implicitly agreeing to cooperate with each other—hence, they are both abiding by what Grice calls the *cooperative principle*.

This may seem obvious enough, but in fact, not all verbal interactions between people are conversations in the technical sense that we are using the term *conversation* here. An interrogation, for instance, is not a conversation. If the law gives me the option, I may decline to engage altogether (in the American context, I may "plead the Fifth"). Or, if I do decide to engage, I may, under the advice of my counsel, engage minimally; I may be instructed not to lie, for instance, but I am not instructed to go out of my way to keep the other side from reaching the wrong conclusion, if the wrong conclusion works in my favor. I could stick to answering the letter of the question, for instance, or I may decide not to use specific terms and I will make the other side work hard to ask me to clarify myself when I am being cagey.

---

3 Randy Allen Harris, *Voice Interaction Design* (Morgan Kaufmann, 2005), 75–126.

In contrast, during a conversation, we are expected to cooperate with each other. I will tell you the truth and only the truth; I will give you as much information as would reasonably be expected of me; I will stay on topic; I will speak clearly; and throughout the conversation, my goal, as is yours, is to be helpful and to advance our exchange forward.

How is this useful in the context of an interaction between a human and voicebot? At a basic level, understanding that a user enters a conversation with a voicebot with the intent to cooperate should prime the product manager and the designer to work hard to ensure that conversations with voicebots have a very well-defined purpose and goal. If one engages a voicebot to cooperate, then they are coming to the voicebot with a problem or goal they want to accomplish and they want the voicebot to help them solve that problem or accomplish that goal. In other words, a successful conversation is one where the participants have managed to cooperate with each other to accomplish a goal. If no goal was accomplished, because that goal was not well-defined, then the conversation was as much of a waste of time as if there were a set of goals, but the voicebot was just not designed well enough to engage the human competently and effectively.

Also, by understanding this basic fact—that the cooperative principle is guiding conversations—a designer should spend the bulk of their energies designing for users who enter their conversation with voicebots with the intention to cooperate. Those are the users the designer should care about the most. Interactions where the user is not cooperating—for instance, they are asking for things that are clearly out of scope—should be identified and dealt with quickly (for instance, connect such uncooperative users to a human being, provide them with information on how to reach a human being, or obtain additional information and then try to quickly wrap up the conversation).

The Maxim of Quality

When I engage you in a conversation, I expect you to: (1) speak truthfully (i.e., not lie); (2) make assertions only to the extent that you believe they are true, and therefore to tell me when you think you are not sure about something; and (3) avoid saying things that would obviously lead me to draw the wrong conclusions.

How is this useful in the context of voicebots? At the most basic level, the voicebot should speak truthfully. Again, this may sound like a truism, but it is not, given the many deployed voicebots that make promises they don't keep. For instance, if the user asks to speak to a human agent and the voicebot signals to the user that they are about to connect them with one, the voicebot should do exactly that instead of, say, transferring them to another voicebot. An example of this that unfortunately happens too often in IVR (interactive voice response) systems is when an IVR of a department within a large organization (say, a bank) determines that the caller can be better served by another department, so the IVR transfers the caller to another IVR when the caller had asked for a human.

The Maxim of Quantity

Here, my expectation is that the voicebot will give me as much information as I need, but not more than I need.

Instead of:

> USER: Is Panera Bread open today?
>
> VOICEBOT: Yes.

Use:

> USER: Is Panera Bread open today?
>
> VOICEBOT: Yes, Panera Bread is open today until 9 p.m.

By the same token, I expect the voicebot not to give me information I don't need for the purposes of the conversation at hand.

Instead of:

> USER: Is Panera Bread open today?
>
> VOICEBOT: Yes, Panera Bread is open today until 9 p.m. Tomorrow, Sunday, they are open from 12 noon to 7 p.m.; and on weekdays, from 12 noon until 8 p.m.

Use:

> USER: Is Panera Bread open today?
>
> VOICEBOT: Yes, Panera Bread is open today until 9 p.m.

The Maxim of Relevance

In addition to expecting the voicebot to give me truthful information and just enough information (not significantly more or less than what we both know is needed) to keep the conversation moving along, I also expect the voicebot to talk about things that are relevant: that is, things that make sense in the sequence of our exchange.

Instead of:

> USER: Is Panera Bread open today?
>
> VOICEBOT: Yes, Panera Bread is open today until 9 p.m. By the way, Amazon Photos storage is now available for a 25% discount to all Amazon Prime members.

Use:

> USER: Is Panera Bread open today?
>
> VOICEBOT: Yes, Panera Bread is open today until 9 p.m.

The Maxim of Manner

Here, the concern is with the language used to communicate the content: the voicebot may be truthful, may be saying as much as it needs to and no more, and may be right on topic, but if it uses terms that I'm not familiar with, then the voicebot would be violating the maxim of manner.

Instead of:

> VOICEBOT: Which of the two bills are you inquiring about, S.1511 or H.R.2265?

Use:

> VOICEBOT: Which of the two bills are you inquiring about: "Protecting America's First Responders Act" or the "Financial Exploitation Prevention Act"?

I would also expect the voicebot to be specific to the extent that it can be specific.

Instead of:

> USER: Are there any Thai restaurants nearby?

> VOICEBOT: Yes, there are several Thai restaurants nearby.

Use:

> USER: Are there any Thai restaurants nearby?

> VOICEBOT: I found a few nearby restaurants. There's New Star Asian Bistro, 1.2 miles away on Old Dominion Drive. The second is Chiang Mai Thai Cookhouse, 1.6 miles away on Elm Street. And the third is Esaan Northeastern Thai Cuisine, 2 miles away on Old Chain Bridge Road.

One last note: As we mentioned, core to our philosophy of design is the proposition that it is a mistake to emulate too closely human-to-human conversations when designing for human-to-voicebot conversations. For instance, human beings may very much mind being interrupted and it would be rude to interrupt a human being and unilaterally take the conversational turn away from them. But with a voicebot, this is not the case: if the voicebot is not giving you what you want, you, the human, should interrupt it and set it back on track (or maybe ask it to stop talking). A designer who designs with the assumption that the user will observe the rule of negotiating turn ownership with the voice assistant is not only wasting time designing a sophisticated assistant, but is probably designing for a frustrating experience: will the assistant object and insist on retaining the turn? Will the user be asked to refrain from interrupting next time they do interrupt? Obviously, not.

Grice's paradigm, although constructed to explain human-to-human conversations, does help us devise sound design strategies that will deliver a highly usable voice first interface; for instance, staying on topic, signaling shifts in topic, not speaking too long, not giving unnecessary information—all of these are key ingredients for delivering great voice first experiences.

But at the same time, to be more useful than harmful, Grice's paradigm should be adopted only if one takes it with a proviso in mind—what we are calling the *human-voicebot asymmetry proviso*:

> There will be many instances where it does not make sense for the human to observe human-to-human rules of conversation. The asymmetry proviso consists in the following statement: even if the human is not expected to observe the human-to-human rules of conversation, the voicebot should be. For instance, the human should be able to interrupt the voicebot whenever they want to interrupt it, but the voicebot should not interrupt the human while the human is speaking. The human should be able to quit the conversation whenever they want to and in any way they want to, but the voicebot should not.

CHAPTER 7

The Basic Tenets

While designing your voicebot for high usability, remember the following tenets. They will keep you safe from blind alleys and other UX design binds that are easy to get into if you are not careful but are difficult to recover from.

The Voicebot Is Not a Human

The voicebot is first and foremost a piece of technology and it exists to make the life of a human better. This is obvious, but it is worth stating and keeping in mind. The voicebot is not a human and it should never pretend to be a human or claim the privileges of a human. It can mimic a human and it can lean on the techniques that humans use with each other to communicate effectively. But it should not behave in such a way that the user is fooled into thinking that the voicebot is as sophisticated and as emotionally intelligent as a human.

Here's why. First, there are ethical issues that such a voicebot would introduce. For instance, using politeness protocols, the voicebot could gain the trust of the user to such an extent that the user forgets that the voicebot is merely a tool that a private corporation or a government agency is using. The user then feels comfortable buying things from, or providing sensitive information to, the voicebot who is working on behalf of the entity.

Second, behaving in a way that gives the user the impression that the voicebot is much smarter than it really is would likely result in the user conversing with it in a way that quickly outstrips the linguistic or conversational abilities of the voicebot, or mislead the user into thinking the voicebot can fulfill more requests than it can.

Instead of:

> VOICEBOT: Fairfax Power. This is Nancy. How can I help you?

Use:

> VOICEBOT: [*chime*] Fairfax Power. Which of the following do you want me to help you with? Report a power outage, ask a question about my bill, or something else.

The Voicebot Should Be as Smart as the Data It Has—and No More!

The voicebot should make the most of the information it has about the user and the context of its interaction with that user; it is the designer's responsibility to engage with the product manager and engineers to find out (1) what is readily at their disposal and (2) what *could* be available through additional development that is within the scope and budget of the project. For instance, would the designer be able to tap into the user's preferences? How about the preferences of most users who are engaging with the voicebot? Are there patterns of behavior that can be leveraged to anticipate and interpret the meaning of what users say and do? How about the physical constraints within which the users are interacting with the voicebot, or the social constraints (e.g., someone in the room while the voicebot and user are talking) or the psychological constraints (e.g., user is anxious, angry)?

Let's look at some examples. Assume that there is a power outage and you are reaching out to the Google action on your smartphone that Fairfax Power, your provider, has published. Assume also that Fairfax Power is aware that it is dealing with an extensive power outage (say, after a severe storm).

Instead of:

> USER: Hey Google, launch Fairfax Power.
>
> VOICEBOT: [*chime*] Fairfax Power. Which of the following do you want me to help you with? Report a power outage, ask a question about my bill, or something else.

Use:

> USER: Hey Google, launch Fairfax Power.
>
> VOICEBOT: [*chime*] Fairfax Power. Are you reaching out to report a power outage?

Now assume that things are back to normal. And assume also that Fairfax Power knows that during normal operations, 87% of the requests they receive are from customers asking about their bill.

Instead of:

> USER: Hey Google, launch Fairfax Power.
>
> VOICEBOT: [*chime*] Fairfax Power. Which of the following do you want me to help you with? Report a power outage, ask a question about my bill, or something else.
>
> USER: Yes, I have a question about my bill.

Use:

> USER: Hey Google, launch Fairfax Power.
>
> VOICEBOT: [*chime*]. Fairfax Power. Do you have a question about your bill?
>
> USER: Yes.

The Voicebot Should Be Consistent

The voicebot should not use different words for the same entity in its language with the human. For instance, it should not use the word "ticket" in one place and then later use the word "issue" to refer to the same entity.

Instead of:

> VOICEBOT: What's the six-digit **case** number assigned to your **issue**?
>
> USER: It's 781656.
>
> VOICEBOT: Got it. I see that this **ticket** is being worked on. Expect a resolution within the next 30 minutes. An email will be sent to you as soon as the **issue** has been resolved.

Use:

> VOICEBOT: What's the six-digit number assigned to your **issue**?
>
> USER: It's 781656.
>
> VOICEBOT: Got it. I see that the **issue** is being worked on. Expect a resolution within the next 30 minutes. An email will be sent to you as soon as the **issue** has been resolved.

It should also stick with one voice and only change that voice when it makes sense (for instance, the voicebot is telling a story with multiple characters). It should not change the language register that it uses (for instance, going from formal to informal).

The Voicebot Should Be Transparent

The human should always know if they are speaking with a human, with a voicebot, or with a voicebot assisted by humans behind the scene. Again, setting aside ethical issues, a user who knows they are speaking with a voicebot will probably behave

in a way that will increase the likelihood of a successful interaction than one who thinks they are engaged with a human being.

Instead of:

> VOICEBOT: Hi there. This is Nancy from Fairfax Power. How are you today?
>
> USER: I'm well, and you?
>
> VOICEBOT: Can't complain. So, how can I be of help?

Use:

> VOICEBOT: [*chime*] Fairfax Power. Which of the following do you want me to help you with? Report a power outage, ask a question about my bill, or something else.
>
> USER: I have a question about my bill.

The voicebot should also be transparent about the data it is collecting. For instance, if the voicebot is one that is engaged through a telephone, and it is saving the phone number of the caller or recording the conversation, the user should be informed at the start of the conversation that their caller ID is being stored or that the call is being recorded. In the case of a voicebot that is being used on a smartphone, if the voicebot wishes to save the location of the user, the user should be informed and asked for their permission.

The Voicebot Should Behave Respectfully

The voicebot should never be disrespectful to the user. What does it mean for a voicebot to be respectful to a user?

For instance, the voicebot should respect the user's time by not having them suffer through long prompts, or by telling the user upfront how long they need to wait for an agent, offering the user the option to be called back.

Another example of respectful behavior is respecting the user's freedom. For instance, letting the user opt out if they don't want to interact with the voicebot or letting them get back to the voicebot while waiting.

Telling the human the truth would be another example of respectful behavior. Yes, voicebots have been known to tell untruths. For example, the voicebot should not tell the user that they are going to be connected to a human agent and then have them interact with, say, another voicebot.

An example of disrespectful behavior would be to terminate an interaction unilaterally; the act of ending a conversation unilaterally is the ultimate act of disrespect in the context of conversations. So, always make sure you design your voicebots so that the end of the exchanges does not come across to the human user as a unilateral decision made by the voicebot.

And there are many other examples.

But, in a nutshell, when you are designing, always keep this at the back of your mind: Even if the human user I am designing for understands that the voicebot is a mere machine and doesn't mean to be disrespectful, if the voicebot behaves disrespectfully, would the human feel slighted? If yes, then I need to design some other behavior.

CHAPTER 8

The Extra-Conversational Context

A core pillar to building an effective voicebot is the depth of information the designer of the voicebot possesses about the broader context within which the conversation is taking place. The more the designer knows about, or is able to anticipate, this context when they are designing the voicebot, the more effective an experience they can design and deliver.

To differentiate this type of context from the one we covered in Chapter 5, which dealt with the context of a conversation in progress (for instance, who owns the conversational turn, whether the conversation is active or paused), we are calling this context *extra-conversational*.

Extra-conversational context is information such as: the state of the user, the physical conditions of the conversation, the social context within which the conversation is taking place, the recent context, known individual user patterns from past interactions between a human and the voicebot, and known user-base patterns.

The State of the User

In what follows, we describe six states of the user that a designer should take into consideration when designing a voicebot.

Emotional State

In those scenarios and use cases where we can infer something about the emotional state of the user (experiencing a power outage, inquiring about lab test results), we design with that emotional state in mind. For instance, if users are likely to be agitated or under some stress, a happy, bouncy voice with a cheerful jingle is probably not appropriate. What is needed instead is a serious, low-key voice that echoes the sense of seriousness and urgency the user is probably experiencing.

Linguistic Competence

If the voicebot is in English and the voicebot knows that the user is not a native speaker of the language (for instance, the voicebot is helping students learn the language), the designer should design prompts that avoid using expressions that may not be familiar to nonnatives.

For example, nonnatives are easily tripped up by adverbial particles.

Instead of this:

> VOICEBOT: Please **hold on** one second as I **pull up** your information.

Design this:

> VOICEBOT: Please **wait** while I **get** your information.

Level of Familiarity

When engaging with the voicebot in question, are the users likely to be frequent users of the voicebot or are they infrequent users?

The frequent user knows how to interact with the voicebot: what to say and how to interpret what the voicebot says. The infrequent user will need hand-holding. Build the mechanism that will enable you to track whether the user is new; if the user is not new, their frequency of use of the voicebot, the last time they used the voicebot, and how extensively they used it is all information to use. This will help you avoid annoying the frequent user with information they know and avoid frustrating the infrequent user because you have not provided them with the instructions they need to engage successfully with the voicebot.

With the first time or infrequent user:

> VOICEBOT: [*chime*] Fairfax Power. Which of the following do you want me to help you with? Report a power outage, ask a question about your bill, or something else.
>
> USER: I have a question about my bill.

With a frequent user:

> VOICEBOT: [*chime*] Fairfax Power. Is this about an outage, your bill, or something else?
>
> USER: My bill.

Technical Savviness

Are users at ease with technology or do they come to the voicebot with a general sense of anxiety? "Here we go, one more gadget to deal with!" Knowing this will enable you to not only design a voicebot that is gentle but to also ensure that prior to engaging the voicebot, the person is provided with information that tells them what voicebots are and what they do. Group training sessions and easy-to-follow videos are effective ways to provide such information.

Physical Readiness

Voicebots talk and listen and expect their partners to be able to talk and listen, in a back-and-forth, flowing exchange. So, one of the effective voicebot's concerns should be to monitor if the user is able to talk and listen comfortably. Usually, this information can be gathered through field research, but it can also be inferred from how much difficulty users are having with the voicebot. For example, the user is speaking but the voicebot can't hear them; the user keeps asking the voicebot to repeat because they can't seem to hear what the voicebot is saying (e.g., the environment is noisy; the user is hard of hearing; the user was asked by the voicebot for their credit card number and, since the card wasn't handy, is fumbling to retrieve it and asking the voicebot to repeat in order to buy time for themselves).

Instead of this:

> VOICEBOT: OK. To help you with your bill, I need your account number. Please go ahead and give it to me, one digit at a time.
>
> USER: [*human doesn't speak*]
>
> VOICEBOT: Sorry, I didn't hear you. I need your account number. Please go ahead and give it to me, one digit at a time.

Design this:

> VOICEBOT: OK. To help you with your bill, I need your account number. Are you ready to give it to me?
>
> USER: Er…no. Hang on. I'm getting it.
>
> VOICEBOT: OK, I will wait. When you are ready, just say, "Hey Google, I am ready." [*voicebot plays wait music*]

Task-Relevant Properties

For example, if the voicebot is helping users engage with their bank, it would be useful for the voicebot to determine whether the user is a student with a low balance who usually engages the voicebot to make sure their balance is not dangerously low or a homeowner who never asks about overdraft protection and may instead be interested in refinancing.

The Physical Context

When the voicebot is engaging the user during a noisy interaction (for instance, in a car), the voicebot should try to detect if the user is speaking from an environment where they cannot speak naturally (they would speak loudly to overcome the loudness around them). Usually, this can be inferred by the frequency of "out of scope" events during an interaction: the user is saying something that the voicebot cannot map to anything that it expects to hear. The more such events occur, the more likely the interaction is taking place in a noisy environment. In such cases, the voicebot should explicitly alert the user that the voicebot is not able to hear them well so that the user can act on the voicebot's complaint in cases where the user is able to do something about it (for instance, lower the volume of the music or mute the TV).

Instead of this:

> USER: My account number is 1224314.
>
> VOICEBOT: Sorry, I didn't understand you. What's your account number again?
>
> USER: That's 1224314.
>
> VOICEBOT: Still not getting it. Can you try it one more time?

Design this:

> USER: My account number is 1224314.
>
> VOICEBOT: Sorry, I didn't understand you. What's your account number again?
>
> USER: That's 1224314.
>
> VOICEBOT: Still not getting it. You may be in a noisy environment or perhaps the connection is not good. Would you like to continue?

The Social Context

Unlike most information technologies (smartphones, for instance), smart speakers are often communal devices; many people have access to using the same device—for instance, in the home, the car, a hotel lobby or room, or the office. As a result, given that both the user and the voicebot must speak openly and can be overheard by others, knowing if a given interaction is being heard by other people or by only the person with whom the voicebot is interacting could be a critical piece of information—especially when the information that is being exchanged is private or sensitive. An intelligent designer should tag whatever information they are sharing as sensitive and when tagged as such, should alert the user that it is so and ask them for permission to speak it out loud.

Instead of this:

> VOICEBOT: [*chime*] HMU Grades Gateway. Welcome back, Drew. Which class?
>
> USER: Postmodern Philosophy.
>
> VOICEBOT: I have your final exam result. You have passed with a grade of 93.

Design this:

> VOICEBOT: [*chime*] HMU Grades Gateway. Welcome back, Drew. Which class?

USER: Postmodern Philosophy.

VOICEBOT: Your final exam result is ready. Do you want me to say it to you out loud now?

USER: No.

VOICEBOT: OK. I have sent you an email with instructions on how to access your result.

The Recent Context

An easy source of information the voicebot can leverage is the actions the user may have taken or events that may have happened that are relevant to the conversation between the voicebot and the human. Here are some examples:

- The user just took an exam and the result of that exam is ready. Knowing this, the voicebot may offer to provide them with those results.

- The user recently logged a new trouble ticket. Knowing this, the voicebot may volunteer to give the user information about that ticket.

- The user's bank balance is running low or there was an overdraft. Knowing this, the voicebot may alert the user and offer to sign them up to the overdraft protection program.

- The user just downgraded or canceled the service. Knowing this, the voicebot may give the user a special offer to upgrade or resubscribe.

Instead of this:

VOICEBOT: [*chime*] HMU Grades Gateway. Welcome back, Drew. Which class?

USER: Postmodern Philosophy.

VOICEBOT: Your final exam result is ready. Do you want me to say it to you out loud now?

USER: Yes.

VOICEBOT: You have passed with a grade of 93.

Design this:

VOICEBOT: [*chime*] HMU Grades Gateway. Welcome back, Drew. Your Postmodern Philosophy exam result is in. Do you want me to say it to you out loud now?

USER: Yes.

VOICEBOT: You have passed with a grade of 93.

User Patterns

A rich and actionable source of information is the pattern of behavior a user has followed in the past, especially behavior that is time related. For instance, if the user engages the voicebot every Saturday morning to find out what their balance is, then whenever the user engages the voicebot on a Saturday morning, the voicebot could offer the user the option of helping them obtain their balance in the opening prompt.

On Saturdays with this particular user, instead of this:

VOICEBOT: [*chime*] First Capital. I can help you check your balance, transfer funds, or something else.

USER: Check balance.

VOICEBOT: From which account, checking, savings, or money market?

USER: Savings.

Design this:

VOICEBOT: [*chime*] First Capital. Do you want me to give you your savings balance?

USER: Yes.

User-Base Patterns

Another rich and actionable source of information is the data that other users have been engaging with the voicebot about. Such information is readily available and, if used judiciously, could delight the user.

An example: If during Sunday mornings, the majority of interactions between users and the voicebot pertain to store hours, the voicebot can offer users that information before moving with the usual menu offer.

On Sundays, with all users, instead of this:

> VOICEBOT: [*chime*] Two-Dollar Store. I can give you the address of our location, our hours, or connect you with someone. Which one would you like?
>
> VOICEBOT: Store hours.
>
> USER: Our hours today are from 10 a.m. to 6 p.m. Do you need anything else?
>
> USER: No.

Design this:

> VOICEBOT: [*chime*] Two-Dollar Store. Our hours today are from 10 a.m. to 6 p.m. Anything else?
>
> USER: No.

CHAPTER 9

The UI Use Case Fit

We all know how crucial the product-market fit is to the viability, let alone the success, of a product. Build a product that is a natural fit for tween girls, market it to busy moms, and you will likely end up with a failed product, no matter how sweet the product or how slick and well-financed the marketing push.

In fact, the number one mistake that startups make is neglecting this basic first step: they start building something with a vague notion, if any, of who the ideal target user is, and then delve into the fun work of ideating and building features and creating lots of cool bells and whistles; then they launch to the world at large, expecting it to embrace their beautiful baby. Often, they neglect to delve into fundamental questions such as: Who is the target user? What problem are we solving for such users (or what additional value are we bringing to their life)? And how are we going to monetize the value we are delivering for them, and do so to the extent that will enable us to survive and thrive as a company (i.e., price the product so the company is profitable)?

A parallel mistake often made by builders of voice experiences is building a voicebot without first asking the basic question: Is the voicebot a good fit for the use case? Instead, many builders delve into the hard work of designing and coding up their voicebot, laboring under the unspoken assumption that given any use case, if a GUI experience exists for that use case (a website, a text-based chatbot, a visual-tactile mobile app), then an experience can and should be built for voice. That is, one should go ahead and build "the equivalent/parallel" voice version of the other non-voice experiences.

In Chapter 4, we touched on the three core characteristics of VUI: time linearity, unidirectionality, and invisibility. We argued that these dimensions are unique to the voice user interface and that they could present a challenge to designers who build graphical/tactile interfaces if they don't keep them in mind. In fact, many novice voicebot designers view these characteristics as weaknesses, or challenges, and point to them as the main reasons why voice user interfaces are unpleasant and unpopular among users.

We believe that such a stand betrays a fundamental flaw in thinking: interfaces cannot be fully described by simply enumerating a list of properties (time linear, unidirectional, ephemeral). These interfaces also need to be described in terms of *what users can do with them*. In fact, to really get to the heart of the matter, we need to talk about not only the properties of these interfaces and what users can do with them but also—and perhaps most important—what users *want to do with them*, their intentions, while using those interfaces. It is only when we have identified a specific use case—the user who comes to the situation with a set of attributes (for instance, they are preparing food, or typing, or lying in bed with their eyes closed) and a set of intentions (they wish to memorize facts, or listen to music, or hear the latest quotes for certain stocks they care about, or turn off the lights) that we can identify how well the voice user interface will perform as a tool that may or may not enable the user to complete their task.

An Illustrative Use Case

Following is a use case to illustrate what we mean. When we are trying to memorize something (a list of facts, a poem, a proverb), we usually do it in a repetitive back and forth, where we speak or mouth what we are trying to memorize and get feedback as to whether we are correct or not, hoping that, in the next try, we will get it right. Ideally, we are working with someone else who is asking us questions while we pace back and forth, giving answers and receiving feedback, and then moving on to the next one. Ideally, the back-and-forth is time-constrained (answer me quickly), we are moving on to the next question linearly, and our eyes are closed (which we naturally often do when we are memorizing). In other words, the "interface" is time linear, unidirectional, and invisible.

The voice first conversational user interface, being time linear, unidirectional, and invisible, would be in such a use case an effective tool for enabling the user to fulfill their want (to memorize something).

In this case, the voice first conversational user interface is powerful *because* it is ephemeral, because it demands the user's attention, requires them to speak up, be constantly present (not wander off), to engage in a focused way. If one wants an interface that lets the user wander off once in a while, or not pay close attention to what is asked of them, or not respond quickly (take their time), then the conversational voice first interface is *not* a fit. No matter how talented the VUI designer is or how many usability magic tricks they use, the experience will be poor. Good examples of use cases that do not fit the conversational voice interface are booking a trip, following the steps of a cooking recipe, finding out what movies are playing in the mall, or answering a 10-question survey. VUI designers can no doubt craft highly usable VUIs, but given the choice between a tablet and a voicebot, users will select the tablet every time—unless, of course, they are not able to use the tablet for whatever reason (they can't see, can't touch, etc.).

The bottom-line point really is this: if you want to build a great voicebot and you want to deliver truly new value, develop a bias for those use cases where no interface, no matter how rich, can beat the voice-only interface.

Basic Heuristics

Here are 14 basic heuristics that should be of use in at least 2 ways:

- They can help you think of use cases where a voicebot will deliver a compelling experience that is superior to one delivered by other interfaces (for instance, visual-tactile mobile apps).

- They may help you assess how good a voicebot will be for a given use case.

The first way is useful to you if you are an entrepreneur and looking to come up with a business idea. The second is useful to you if you are a product manager or designer looking to understand how much work you will need to do to bridge the gap between the use case and the UI.

The more of these heuristics that are answered yes, the more compelling your voicebot will be:

- The user is not able to or does not want to use their hands.

- The user is not able to or does not want to use their eyes.

- The user can easily respond quickly when it is their turn to speak.

- It is desirable for the user to be forced to respond quickly when it is their turn to speak.

- The user is able to listen carefully to what is being said to them.

- It is desirable for the user to be forced to listen carefully to what is being said to them.

- The user is able to speak up.
- It is desirable for the user to speak up.
- The user can easily enunciate clearly.
- It is desirable to force the user to enunciate clearly.
- The user can easily remain focused.
- It is desirable to force the user to remain focused.
- The user is able to be patient and is not in a hurry.
- It is desirable that the user is forced to be patient.

Note that the above-mentioned use case of the user who wishes to memorize facts without looking or touching anything—the target user—complies with each of the 14 heuristics.

CHAPTER 10

The Elements of Starting

You get only one shot at making a good first impression.

With voicebots, such an impression is formed by users and conveyed by VUI designers with the conversation's opening sequence. The following sections give you tips to help you craft an effective opening prompt.

Be Brief

Belabored, verbose opening prompts confirm the worst stereotype of the dumb, overbearing voicebot. If you force users to listen to 30 seconds of instructions, information, and disclaimers before they can take the first step toward solving their problem, you will not only have started on the wrong note but would have given the user a whole 30 seconds to change their mind and terminate the conversation. Every single word in your opening prompt needs to be indispensable. If you can get rid of a word without losing meaning or effectiveness, do it.

Use an Audio Icon

A well-crafted, distinctive, pleasant audio icon—or, even better, an audio icon that the user is familiar with and is likely to associate with the brand that the voicebot represents—played at the very start of an interaction is not only an effective way of signaling to users that they are interacting with a voicebot and not a human, but also a good way of communicating to users that the voicebot was designed and crafted with care. The implication is that the brand they are engaging with cares about its customers and will work hard to ensure that customers are satisfied. This starts the interaction on a positive note upon which further experiences can build for usability.

Drop the "Welcome to..."

Instead of using the perfunctory "Welcome to...," simply have the voicebot announce the brand's name, preceded or followed by an audio icon, and then followed by the company's tagline, if the company has one. Such an opening will not only set your voicebot apart from the usual ones but also will have shortened the length of your prompt.

Instead of:

> VOICEBOT: Welcome to Widget Solutions, where intelligence is at your service.

Try:

> VOICEBOT: [*chime*] Widget Solutions. Intelligence at your service.

Or:

> VOICEBOT: Widget Solutions. [*chime*] Intelligence at your service.

Never Ever Say, "Please Listen Carefully as Our Options Have Changed"

This is an awful invention and it must be banned once and for all. Upon hearing it, the user will immediately think of the old style "phone tree," and that is not a good association.

Have the Voicebot Refer to Itself in the First Person

Empirical studies have shown that users like to have the voice-bot refer to itself with the personal "I" rather than the impersonal "assistant" or "system" or "skill."[1]

Instead of:

> VOICEBOT: This skill tells you what state a zip code belongs to.

Try:

> VOICEBOT: I can tell you what state a zip code belongs to.

Drop "You Can Interrupt Me at Any Time"

As we have argued in the Introduction, we advocate for the establishment of a new world order where the VUI designer does not feel it is their responsibility to educate the user on the basics of engaging with a voicebot. In addition to being able to say "Repeat" to have the voicebot repeat what they just said, or "Skip" to go to the next item when the voicebot is speaking an enumerated list of items (e.g., summary of news stories), users should be able to interrupt voicebots at any time.

Keep the Origination Context in Mind

If at all possible, keep in mind the context users may be starting from in their interaction with the voicebot and the assumptions they are likely to make about those interactions.

---

1 Susan J. Boyce, "Natural Spoken Dialogue Systems for Telephony Applications," *Communications of the ACM* 43, no. 9 (2000): 29–34.

For instance, if the human is engaging the voicebot in reaction to an ad that said, "To place your order, just say, 'Hey Google, Talk to the Mighty Green Grill'":

Instead of:

> VOICEBOT: [*chime*] Grills Are Us! Which one would you like to order: the Mega Red Grill, the Mighty Green Grill, or the Sturdy Blue Grill?

Try:

> VOICEBOT: [*chime*] Grills Are Us! Are you ready to order the Mighty Green Grill?

Remember the User's Preferences

If the voicebot is able to identify the user (for instance, their smart speaker device ID or the telephone number they are calling from) and has a record of their language preference, then the voicebot should drop the language question and simply proceed with the language preference it has on record.

Another example would be asking them for their frequent flyer number or member ID.

Of course, should the user need to access sensitive information or execute transactions, a layer of protection needs to be introduced (for instance, asking them for a PIN code).

Anticipate User-Specific Requests

Similarly, if the user has recently placed an order from the brand's website or mobile app, then they are probably engaging the voicebot to find out about the status of that order. If safely providing the user with such information in the opening prompt does not take more than a few seconds, then have the voicebot volunteer the information before offering the standard main menu. Or, at the very least, ask them if that is why they are engaging with the voicebot.

Instead of:

> VOICEBOT: [*chime*] Grills Are Us! I see that you have placed a Mighty Green Grill order with us. Do you want to find out the status of the order?
>
> USER: Yes.
>
> VOICEBOT: OK. Your order is about to be shipped to the 6505 address. Anything else?
>
> USER: No.

Try:

> VOICEBOT: [*chime*] Grills Are Us! Just so you know, your Mighty Green Grill order is about to be shipped to the 6505 address. Anything else?
>
> USER: No.

Anticipate General User-Base Requests

In addition to leveraging specific information about the user, the voicebot should also leverage information about the user base as a whole.

For example, your customers are launching your voicebot to report a service outage and are overwhelmingly selecting the "technical support" option. If the voicebot is experiencing such a spike on a specific menu option across users, then have the voicebot adjust its behavior to offer that option first before presenting users with the standard main menu (e.g., "Do you want technical support?") Again, the voicebot—and therefore the brand—will come across as smart and proactive, and in the case of an outage, the customer will immediately feel better knowing that the company is aware of the outage and is therefore working on it. All in all, your brand will be perceived as being on top of things. The voicebot should of course revert to the pre-outage menu behavior when the request spike subsides.

CHAPTER 11

The Elements of Prompting

Writing prompts can be tricky. When you design your voice-bot, don't leave the final wording of your prompts until the very end. Instead, invest at the outset in the careful crafting of your prompts and make sure you test, review, and revise, until you get the wording just right.

This chapter provides key tips to help you write effective prompts. Following the advice we give you, however, should not replace testing your voicebots end-to-end and listening carefully to how the prompts sound *in context* and how real users react to them. Do both and you will see a marked improvement in your voicebot's usability.

Prompt Types

Following are the basic prompt types you will need to write:

Providing information
 The voicebot responds with some piece of information.

Requesting information
 The voicebot asks the user to provide a piece of information. For example, "What is your birth date?" or "Say or enter your credit card number."

Confirming information

There are two types of confirmation prompts, explicit and implicit. In an explicit confirmation, the prompt echoes back the information it thought it was given by the user and explicitly requests a yes/no answer to its explicit confirmation request. In an implicit confirmation, the voicebot echoes back the information without requesting any confirmation feedback.

Offering choices

Multiple turn interactions with voicebots almost always necessitate the voicebot asking the user to make a choice between several options. Doing this in such a way that the user understands the choices and is able to act on them is what we will examine in Chapter 12.

Signaling an error condition

Prompts that signal to the user that an error has occurred and guide users back to the right track are crucial to the usability of a voicebot. Chapter 13 offers some rules and guidelines for designing effective error strategies.

Writing Effective Prompts

Here we provide 15 tips on how to write effective prompts.

Use Language That Is Commonly Used in Conversations

Don't be tempted with formal, cramped language, or language that reads nicely but would sound heavy in a conversational interaction.

Here is a bad prompt:

> VOICEBOT: Please tell me the date of your birth, including the month, day, and year.

Here is a better prompt:

> VOICEBOT: What's your birthday? For instance, June 1st, 1991.

Remember That the User Will Mimic the Voicebot

When you design your prompts, keep in mind that the user will be listening carefully to the language spoken by the voicebot. If the voicebot uses stiff or verbose language, so will the user. If the voicebot is natural sounding and to the point, so will the user be; the user will also closely mimic the very wording used by the voicebot.[1] If the voicebot uses the word *ticket* to refer to trouble cases, the user will mimic it and will use that word.

The smartest strategy is to do your research upfront and to find out what kind of language users actually use. For example, if you have call recordings between customers and contact center agents, listen to those conversations and map out the language that users use. If you do this, you will end up building a voicebot that uses a language that users are likely to find easy to understand and pick up.

Unless It's Essential to the Use Case, Don't Use Slang or Jargon

Jargon is by definition a circumscribed subset of a larger language. It is code that designates a group of people as the in-crowd and the rest as outsiders. Unless only the in-crowd is expected to interact with the voicebot, avoid using idiomatic slang or jargon.

---

1 For a discussion on mimicking, see Randy Allen Harris, "Stealth Training," in *Voice Interaction Design* (Morgan Kaufmann, 2005), 360–61.

Put the Most Important Information First

When providing requested information, put the most important elements of the voicebot's response at the beginning of the prompt. (And "important" is what the user wants to hear first, not what the company wants the user to hear first.) Otherwise, you will risk having the user interrupt the prompt and miss the important information they were seeking.

Not good:

> VOICEBOT: We have a Smucker's special: buy two, get one for free. Jams and jellies can be found in Aisle 15.

Better:

> VOICEBOT: Jams and jellies can be found in Aisle 15. By the way, we have a Smucker's special: buy two, get one for free.

Use Want Instead of Wish

A voicebot does not exist to grant wishes. It exists to determine wants and fulfill them.

Not good:

> VOICEBOT: What do you wish to do next?

Better:

> VOICEBOT: What do you want to do next?

Avoid Using Speak

Bad prompt:

> VOICEBOT: Please speak the number of bedrooms in your house.

Good prompt:

> VOICEBOT: How many bedrooms are there in your house?

Use Contractions

People use contractions unless they want to make a point by dropping the contraction. A voicebot that systematically doesn't use contractions will sound robotic and distant.

Bad prompt:

> VOICEBOT: I am sorry, I cannot hear you.

Good prompt:

> VOICEBOT: Sorry, I can't hear you.

Note that if the voicebot uses contractions by default, then you will be able to place emphasis when you need to by dropping a contraction. For example:

> VOICEBOT: Sorry, I still *cannot* hear you.

Be Consistent in Your Wording

Don't use different words to describe your objects or properties—for example, pick either "ticket" or "case," "agent" or "representative," "invalid" or "incorrect," "log in" or "check in," and stick to the choices you pick for both how the voicebot speaks to the user and how you want the user to respond to voicebot requests.

Avoid Mixing Recorded and TTS Speech

Unless you have no choice, avoid mixing recorded prompts with automated, computer-spoken, text-to-speech (TTS). A "hybrid" prompt will always sound jarring, and often even more jarring than a straight TTS prompt. Someone listening to a prompt that starts off in a pleasant human voice will not be straining their ear to carefully listen for a sudden burst of TTS. Chances are that a hybrid prompt will need to be repeated, and at the very least, the designer should offer the user the option of repeating the prompt.

It's OK for a Sentence to End in a Preposition

If the more natural sounding way of asking a question or providing information has you ending a sentence with a preposition, so be it. Do not twist sentences into weird-sounding phraseologies just to satisfy some outdated English grammar rule that, in any case, is almost always disregarded in spoken speech.

Here is a not-so-natural-sounding prompt:

> VOICEBOT: From where will you be leaving?

Here is the better prompt:

> VOICEBOT: Where are you leaving from?

Avoid Using Whom

It's bad enough when a person says it in a conversational setting. It's even worse when a voicebot uses it.

Minimize the Use of Please

A sequence of voicebot requests all starting with "Please" will not make the voicebot sound polite. It will make it sound needlessly repetitive. Don't turn "please" into a meaningless prefix to your requests. Use it sparingly so that it retains its effect.

Use Incremental Prompts When Dealing with Expert Users

The idea behind using what are called *incremental prompts* is to initially provide the user with minimal guidance as to what to use, and only upon failure provide them with a more elaborate explanation of what is expected of them.

For example, a stock quote voicebot could bluntly open with "Hot Stocks. [*some audio*] Which stock?" If the user does not respond within some timeout period, the voicebot could then come back with "You can say, IBM, Microsoft, Google, or Apple."

Incremental prompts are used when the default user is expected to be an expert, repeat user of the voicebot. For instance, if most users are going to know what to say at the main menu, it is best to open with a succinct prompt and introduce a more explicit language only when necessary.

Use Tapering Prompts to Minimize on Wordy Repetitions

As a general rule, you don't want your voicebot to be needlessly redundant and repetitive, whether within a prompt or across the call. A voicebot that robotically repeats itself is exhausting to listen to, if for no other reason than because it is wasting time.

Needlessly wordy:

> VOICEBOT: IBM is trading at 52.15 dollars, up 1.2. Microsoft is trading at 67.51 dollars, up 0.7. Apple is trading at 37.78 dollars, up 2.67.

Better:

> VOICEBOT: IBM is trading at 52.15 dollars, up 1.2; Microsoft at 67.51, up 0.7; and Apple at 37.78, up 2.67.

Needlessly wordy:

> VOICEBOT: How satisfied are you with our responsiveness? Give me a score from 1 to 5.
>
> USER: 3.
>
> VOICEBOT: How satisfied are you with our cleanliness? Give me a score from 1 to 5.
>
> USER: 4.

Using tapering:

> VOICEBOT: How satisfied are you with our responsiveness? Give me a score between 1 and 5.
>
> USER: 3.

VOICEBOT: How about our cleanliness?

USER: 4.

Request an Explicit Confirmation Only When Necessary

Requesting that every bit of information the user provides be confirmed will, at the very least, annoy the user. You should use explicit confirmation in the following situations:

- The information you are collecting is "crucial" (e.g., amount of money to be transferred).
- The voicebot is about to execute an action that may be costly to undo (e.g., canceling a reservation).

CHAPTER 12

Choices

Primitive as it may seem, the old-fashioned linear menu remains one of the most effective ways to elicit information from users in conversational voice interfaces. The voicebot offers a list of options, the user picks what they want, and the voicebot moves on to the next step. Nothing could be more straightforward. And yet, one can easily design a difficult-to-use menu unless some basic principles are observed. This chapter gives you some guidelines to help you design usable menus.

Present the Most Requested Items First

Not all menu items are created equal. If you know which items are requested most frequently, place those items at the top of the menu list. This way, by definition, most users will spend little time waiting for the menu item that they wish to select.

Keep the Menu List to Three Items or Less

Because of the invisible nature of the voice first interface, try to keep your menus to three items or less. In case you need to present the user with more than three items, split the list into two, with the first two items on the list presenting the user with the items they are most likely to request, and access to the second list offered with the third option.

Keep the Menu Depth to Three Levels or Less

People don't like deep menus. Deep menus force users to keep a mental map of their interaction. And the deeper the menu, the stronger the feeling they have of being led into a blind alley, with little hope to get to where they want to go. If you can't keep your menu's depth to three or less, go back to the drawing board and see if you can't consolidate some of those tree branches.

Avoid the Construction of "for/to X, Say X; for/to Y, Say Y; for/to Z, Say Z"

Simply rewrite the menu prompt as, "What would you like? You can say *X*, *Y*, or *Z*"; or "What would you like, *X*, *Y*, or *Z*?"

For example, instead of this:

> VOICEBOT: What would you like to do next? To get your current balance, say, "Check balance"; to open a new account, say, "Open account"; to transfer funds from one account to another, say, "Transfer funds."

Write this:

> VOICEBOT: "What would you like to do next: check your balance, open an account, or transfer funds from one account to another?"

Don't Use, "Please Select from the Following Options"

A tired phrase that needs to be retired.

Use the Same Part of Speech/Clausal Form When Listing Menu Options

Bad prompt:

> VOICEBOT: You can say, "Balance," "Open," or "Transfer."

Good prompt:

> VOICEBOT: You can say, "Check balance," "Open account," or "Transfer funds."

Better still:

> VOICEBOT: What would you like to do, check your balance, open an account, or transfer funds?

Let Users Ask, "What Are My Choices?"

At any point in the conversation, the user should be able to ask, "What are my choices?" In response, the voicebot should respond by positioning the user in the conversation and then listing the options that are available to the user:

> USER: What are my choices?
>
> VOICEBOT: We were transferring funds. I need to know which account you would like to transfer funds from. You can say, "Checking," "Savings," or "Money Market."

Let Users "Climb Back" the Menu

Unless a transaction that cannot be easily undone has been executed, the user should be able to say, "go back" and then be placed at the menu that preceded the one where they found themselves when they said, "go back":

> VOICEBOT: What would you like to do, check your balance, withdraw funds, or transfer funds?
>
> USER: Transfer funds.

VOICEBOT: Transferring funds. Which account do you want to transfer funds from, checking, savings, or money market?

USER: Go back.

VOICEBOT: Back to the main menu. What would you like to do: check your balance, withdraw funds, or transfer funds?

Offer to Repeat the Menu Options After a 3-Second Pause

If the user does not respond to a menu offer within 3 seconds, chances are that they are confused about what to do or need more time to decide. Offering to repeat the options is a good way to get them back on track.

Turn on Barge-In for Expert Users

If your voicebot is going to be engaged repeatedly or regularly by users, make sure you design your prompts and menus so that those users who know what to say are able to swiftly traverse the menus and are not forced to interact with the voicebot at the pace of a novice. Crucial to accomplishing this is turning on the barge-in setting while playing menu prompts.

If you find yourself having to turn off barge-in because your usability studies or logs are showing you that people are making erroneous menu choices, then you may want to look into how you are listing your menu items. Perhaps you are listing rarely requested choices first, and users are mistaking those items for the choices they want to make—or perhaps the wordings you are using to describe items are easily confused with one another.

Include and Teach Shortcuts

If you want your users to start loving your voicebot, teach them how to skip prompts and menus to get where they want to be. The most effective way to accomplish this is to teach them shortcuts.

Two things to remember about shortcuts. First, know *when* to provide them. The best place to play a shortcut instruction is during the time the user is made to wait for a transaction to complete. Second, provide them sparingly. During a user interaction, provide no more than one shortcut instruction. For example:

VOICEBOT: What would you like to do: check balance, withdraw funds, or transfer funds?

USER: Transfer funds.

VOICEBOT: Transferring funds. Which account do you want to transfer funds from: checking, savings, or money market?

USER: Savings.

VOICEBOT: And which account do you want to transfer funds to: checking or money market?

USER: Checking.

VOICEBOT: OK. Transferring from savings to checking. How much money would you like to transfer?

USER: 200 dollars.

VOICEBOT: 200 dollars from savings to checking. It will take me a few seconds to execute the transaction. Please hold. And by the way, next time you want to do a similar transfer, you can just say, "Transfer from savings to checking."

CHAPTER 13

Managing Failure

The quality of a voicebot is judged not only by how the voicebot manages its interactions with users when everything is going smoothly, but also (and perhaps more importantly) by how it navigates situations when things don't proceed as expected.

In this chapter, we discuss recovery strategies that, if systematically observed, will markedly improve a voicebot's performance and, therefore, the satisfaction of its users.

Types of Failure

First, let's describe the four main types of failure that a user may encounter while engaging with a voicebot.

No-Input

A *no-input* failure is triggered when the voicebot is unable to detect sound from the user.

No-Match

A *no-match* failure is triggered when the voicebot is unable to interpret what the user said. In other words, the voicebot heard the user say something that the voicebot did not expect them to say.

Misrecognition

A *misrecognition* failure occurs when the voicebot thinks the user said something that is different from what the user actually said. Unlike the no-input and the no-match failures, misrecognition is a failure that the voicebot is not aware of. Two situations then present themselves: (1) The user is able to quickly detect that the voicebot misrecognized what the user said, or (2) The user does not detect that the voicebot misrecognized what the user said.

System Failure

A *system* failure occurs when something goes wrong at the application layer. For instance, a data source is not available.

Causes of Failure

Next, we discuss some of the potential causes of voicebot failures. This list is by no means exhaustive, and a good designer will always be on the lookout for any additional causes of failure that may be particular to the use case for which they are designing.

No-Input

A no-input failure usually happens when the user is confused and does not know what to say. There are also situations where the user is simply pausing to think about what they want to say or how they want to formulate their request. Or they may just be taking their time thinking how to respond. The prompt should accordingly provide helpful information to direct the user on what to do. A prompt that simply says, "Sorry, I didn't hear anything," is not helpful. A more helpful prompt would be one that said something like, "Please give me your account number. You can also say, 'Hang on' if you need more time or, 'Help,' for more instructions."

No-Match

This usually happens when the user does not fully understand what the voicebot is expecting them to say, whether because the user said something that is just not relevant or because the language that was designed and implemented for the voicebot was not designed well.

In either case, a prompt that simply says, "Sorry, I didn't understand that" is not helpful. A more helpful prompt would say, "Sorry, I didn't understand that. I just need your account number. You can speak it one digit at a time. If you need more time just say, 'Hang on.'"

Misrecognition

A misrecognition usually occurs when elements in the language models of the various intents the user can communicate are similar to one another. For example, if the user is able to communicate the intent of continuing the conversation by saying "Hang on," and the intent of terminating the conversation by saying "Hang up," chances are that the voicebot will hear one thing instead of the other and do exactly the opposite of what the user intended the voicebot to do.

System

Back-end failures have many causes. For instance, a service that the voicebot relies on to execute its interactions fails. An example would be the service that enables the voicebot to retrieve the latest stock price is not responding or is responding with a failure code (for instance, no data is available). Another cause of failure may be that the software running the voicebot has a bug; for example, it crashes because it divides something by zero, or it is trying to add a number to a character.

Best Practices

Having enumerated the types of conversational failure and some of the main causes of such failures, we now propose 10 best practices for how to deal with voicebot failures.

Always Have the Voicebot Take the Blame

Never imply, let alone explicitly state, that the user has done or is doing something wrong or that the failure is their fault. Users are under enough pressure trying to figure out how to interact with the voicebot. Having that voicebot wave a scolding finger at them will result mainly in the user becoming frustrated and less cooperative.

Here is an example of an accusing prompt:

> VOICEBOT: You have entered an incorrect account number.

Here is a less threatening rewording of that prompt:

> VOICEBOT: Hmm, I can't find that account number.

Give the User Three Chances

Unless you have a good reason to do otherwise, keep the number of no-input and no-match tries to three. After that, if you can point them to another channel, preferably one that gets them interacting with a human being, do that.

Offer Explicit Examples of How to Respond

As mentioned earlier, do take the time to craft your no-input and no-match prompts with the aim of providing users with information that will help them recover. Don't just tell users that the voicebot could not hear or was not able to understand what the user said. Instead, tell them what you expect them to say and how you expect them to say it.

Providing explicit examples of what is expected is usually the best way to elicit the correct wording from users. For instance, upon a no-input or a no-match, instead of simply asking again:

> VOICEBOT: Sorry, I didn't get that. When were you born?

The voicebot should ask:

> VOICEBOT: Sorry, I didn't get that. You can give me your birth date by saying something like, "June 15, 1970."

Be Careful When You Reprompt

Pay attention to the flow of your voicebot's prompts when a no-input or no-match event occurs. Take the following interaction:

> VOICEBOT: Great! And how would you rate our hospitality? You can say, "poor, good, or excellent."
>
> USER: [*silence*]

A careful reprompting would have the voicebot say:

> VOICEBOT: Sorry, I didn't hear you. How would you rate our hospitality? You can say, "poor, good, or excellent."

A less careful reprompting would have the voicebot say:

> VOICEBOT: Sorry, I didn't hear you. Great! And how would you rate our hospitality? You can say, "poor, good, or excellent."

The failure in the second formulation consists in using the same prompt that was used upon initial entry for the post no-input reentry.

Establish "Safety Points"

A *safety point* is a "location" in the conversation flow to which the user can be taken in case the interaction between the user and the voicebot goes off track and the user finds themselves confused as to what to do next.

If the voicebot has a main menu of options, for instance, that main menu could be a good safety point to take the user back to. With voicebots, users don't mind repeating themselves if they are able to reestablish clarity and get back on track.

Never Terminate a Conversation Unilaterally—Especially During Recovery

When the maximum number of allotted no-input or no-match chances has been reached by the user during an interaction (e.g., they have failed to say something three times in a row to the same voicebot request), don't just stop the conversation. Here are some possible things the voicebot should do:

Take the user to a safety point
> But keep track of the times they have been taken back to that safety point. If this is the second time in a row, pursue one of the other strategies below.

Take the user to a human agent
> By far the best strategy, if you do have agents that you can take the user to.

Just move on
> In cases where the failure to collect the information sought is not a showstopper—e.g., a survey—or when partial data collected from the user is still useful, the voicebot should simply move on to the next step after the final no-input or no-match. In such situations, it is better to continue with the conversation than risk frustrating the user into abandoning the exchange.

Provide the user with useful information
> This helps them accomplish what they wanted to accomplish (e.g., give them a special support line they could try, point them to a specific page on the website, give them an email address, etc.).

Don't Be Repetitive During Recovery

Repeating, "I am sorry I didn't understand that. Please give me your seven-digit account number," after three no-matches in a row is like saying to the user, "You are stupid, and I am going to repeat my request until it gets through your thick skull!"

Make sure that each phrasing in a sequence of no-matches requests information in a different way and provides the user with additional help to get them to say the right thing.

Orient the User About Where They Are

Sometimes, users become tongue-tied or don't know what to say for the simple reason that they have become disoriented and no longer know where they are in the interaction. This is especially true during interactions that take the user down a multilevel menu. Upon a no-input failure, it usually helps to briefly indicate to the user the context of the interaction they are engaged in. For example:

> VOICEBOT: What would you like to do? You can check your balance, withdraw funds, or transfer funds.
>
> USER: Transfer funds.
>
> VOICEBOT: From which account: checking, savings, or money market?
>
> USER: [*silence*]
>
> VOICEBOT: We were transferring funds. Which account would you like to transfer funds from? You can say, "Checking, Savings, or Money Market."

Give the User Information About the Issue

In cases where the issue is a system failure and therefore neither the voicebot nor the user can do much about fixing it or navigating around it, it is a good practice to design the voicebot in such a way that in addition to signaling to the user that an issue has occurred, the voicebot also provides the human with information that they can easily provide someone who owns the voicebot (for instance, the support team at the business that is using the voicebot with its users). A failure code that the user can easily note down and communicate to Support, that Support can pass on to Engineering, and that Engineering can use to fix the issue, helps everyone. The user will feel they were able to do something about the issue—i.e., communicate a failure code. Support doesn't have to interrogate the user to extract information, and Engineering does not have to interrogate Support.

Do Not Be Overly Apologetic

A voicebot that apologizes a lot is a voicebot that fails a lot. Repeated failure is already an annoyance. Simply apologizing and then continuing on with the failures will annoy the user far more than it will assuage them. The voicebot should be apologetic when it fails, but it should very quickly move to correct the failures or provide the human with a way to reach a human agent who can help them.

CHAPTER 14

Help Strategies

No matter how carefully you design and craft your voicebot, chances are that users will at some point need help interacting with it. They may need help simply because they are novice users of voicebots, or they may need help because at some point in their interaction with your voicebot, they encountered a problem and need some guidance to get the conversation back on track.

The keys to successful help are (1) relevance, (2) actionability, and (3) brevity. Provide help when, and only when, it is needed; provide information the user can act on; and provide only as much information as is needed and not more.

The next sections give you guidelines that should inform your design and implementation of a truly helpful voicebot.

Tell the User That Help Is Available

What good is a help system if the user is not aware that it exists? If you expect a good portion of your voicebot's users to be first-time or infrequent users, let them know from the opening prompt that they can ask for help, and tell them exactly how they can ask for help ("If at any point you need help, just say 'help me.'"). By the same token, If you are able to tell that the user is not engaging the voicebot for the first time, then suppress the language about the existence of help.

Detect When the User Needs Help

A user who is not answering your voicebot's request (no-input) or is answering it with language that the voicebot does not understand (no-match), is probably a confused user and therefore a user in distress and in need of help. Similarly, a user who is responding negatively to requests for confirmation that a task was successfully performed by the voicebot ("Did I answer your question?") is also probably a user who is in need of help. Make sure your voicebot takes note of any such occurrences so it can let the user know they can ask for help.

Structure Your Help

The first step to designing a helpful voicebot is predicting the types of problems people may encounter while using it. Given the linear and constrained nature of voice first interactions, the necessity of coming up with parsimonious, focused help is especially pressing. There is no room for any sloppiness or inefficiency that may be tolerated when interacting with visual, GUI help. When interacting with voicebots, users can't skim and skip to locate what they are looking for. Voice-based help systems that ignore this difference are nearly unusable and will frustrate the user more than they will help them.

So, make sure your help system is not a manual describing what the voicebot can do, but rather a mechanism the user can use to help them with on-the-spot, in-the-flow-of-things, actionable advice that will help them overcome the specific challenge at hand.

Mention the Basic Task the Voicebot Is Trying to Solve

If the user seems confused about why the voicebot exists in the first place, have the voicebot state it clearly: "I am here to give you details on the closest speedy car that is available for you to rent." Sometimes the user is confused because they thought they were engaging a voicebot to help them with something the voicebot is not designed to help them with. Start with that, and don't waste the user's time trying to figure out how to use a voicebot that was not designed to do what the user wants to do.

Offer Help to the Most Frequently Encountered Problems First

As always, leverage the information you have. If you have information about the types of issues that people are having with your voicebot, use that information. If you don't know exactly the nature of the problem, lean on that information: If 80% of the users need more time for a particular question, offer help that assumes that the problem with that question is the problem that 80% of the users are having. For instance, if 80% are quiet after asking them for their account number because they don't have it, when they don't answer, say, "If you need time to locate the account number, just say, 'Hold on.'"

Return from Where You Left Off After Giving Help

Since voicebot interactions are time linear, chances are that after listening to help instructions, the user will need some more help to be reminded where they had left things off before the help interaction started. A simple way to remind the user is by telling them where in the conversation they are now positioned. Usually, a short declarative will suffice: "We are picking the movie you want to buy tickets for," or, "Here again are the movies that are playing in your theater."

Be Concise and Specific with Your Help

Remember that a user seeking help is a user who has had some problem understanding what your voicebot wants them to do. For instance, if your voicebot gave the user a list of items to pick from and the user did not respond in time (no-input), it may be that they didn't understand what the choices were, or they didn't hear the option that they were looking for in the list, or maybe they just need more time. What help the user needs will depend on which of these three states pertains to their situation, and upon detecting the issue, the voicebot can respond in a way that will help the user move along successfully. If the user didn't understand the choices, a prompt explaining the choices is the right kind of help. If the user didn't hear the choice they want to make, a different prompt is probably appropriate. And if they just need more time, then the voicebot needs to give them more time to make their selection.

In any case, when you craft your help prompts, avoid the temptation of turning those prompts into an audio tour showcasing all the things your voicebot can do. Keep your help prompts short and focused on troubleshooting the user's problem.

Use Context to Guide Your Explanations

Context is the best indicator of the type of problem a user is having and, therefore, the kind of help they should be offered. For instance, if a user is having trouble answering a question, start by first offering them a clarification on what the voicebot expects from them by, for example, rephrasing the question more explicitly or by offering an example (see the next section on illustrating your explanations), and only then offer general help to them about using the voicebot.

Illustrate Your Explanations with Examples

Take advantage of the fact that users reflexively mimic the voicebot they interact with. Users will emulate a voicebot's language patterns, its vocabulary, and even the pace of its speech. In the context of providing help, you can exploit this by giving examples of how the user should interact with the voicebot. Instead of simply instructing the user with "Next I need your departure date. Give me the month, followed by the day, and then the year," the voicebot would do better if it added, "What's your departure date? For instance, you can say, October 5th, 2021."

Offer Help Only When It Is Needed

"Helpful" information is annoying noise when the user is not in need of help. Don't offer help about how to navigate the voicebot until such help is needed—give the customer a chance to speak first; for example, after a three-second pause offer, "If you need to hear the options again, say 'Repeat.'"

CHAPTER 15

Verbal Dialogue Marking

A *dialogue marker* is a word or a phrase that plays a role in managing the flow and structure of a dialogue. Examples of dialogue markers are: "Let's start," "First," "Next," "By the way," and "Anyway."

One of the driving tenets of this book is that a voicebot should never pretend to possess human sensibilities. It should never behave in such a way that it somehow tricks the human into thinking the voicebot has feelings. It should not emulate human behavior to such an extent that the human would suspend disbelief, even briefly (in that they would begin to say things they normally wouldn't do if they had remained aware that they were engaging with a voicebot). And why is this important? It is important because this machine is not a *creatio ex nihilo* (creation out of nothing). The voicebot was created by an entity (for instance, a giant tech company) and may not necessarily be looking out for the best interest of the user. For instance, a data-hungry corporation could successfully get the human user to trust the voicebot enough to provide that voicebot with sensitive information just because the voicebot was impeccably polite or endearingly flattering.

By the same token, a voicebot does not need to go to the other extreme and behave so robotically that the behavior gets in the way of an effective dialogue.

Take the following exchange:

> VOICEBOT: How old are you?
>
> USER: Twenty-four.
>
> VOICEBOT: Are you male or female?
>
> USER: Female.
>
> VOICEBOT: What's your home phone number?
>
> USER: 703-555-1234.
>
> VOICEBOT: I am now setting up your account.

Compare it to this exchange:

> VOICEBOT: First, how old are you?
>
> USER: Twenty-four.
>
> VOICEBOT: And are you male or female?
>
> USER: Female.
>
> VOICEBOT: OK. And what's your home phone number?
>
> USER: 703-555-1234.
>
> VOICEBOT: Got it. Thanks. I have what I need. I am now setting up your account.

Clearly, the first exchange is more robotic than the second one, and so one can't accuse the designer of the first exchange of designing a voicebot that aims to trick the user into thinking that the voicebot was a human or had human-level conversational skills. By the same token, it would be fair to say that the second exchange is smoother and flows better. One could even say that it feels "less confrontational" than the first and delivers a more enjoyable experience than the first exchange. In this instance, the second design—the one that is less robotic—is the better design because its flow keeps the user focused. In other words, here's a situation where the designer needs to have an ear for what is effective and make their call accordingly rather than cling to an inflexible principle—in our case, the principle of the voicebot not sounding overly human. The experienced designer should never introduce dialogue markers simply to make a voicebot sound less robotic, but they should also never hesitate to introduce such markers if the markers facilitate the delivery of an exchange that flows naturally.

The next sections present tips on how to use dialogue markers to functionally enhance usability by delivering signals that help the conversation between the human and the voicebot move forward.

Acknowledge Receipt of Information

An important function that dialogue markers fulfill is signaling that the flow of information between the conversational participants is proceeding smoothly. In the context of human-to-voicebot dialogues, where often the exchange consists of the voicebot asking the human for pieces of information, one can very easily end up creating a jarring experience by omitting such markers.

In the previous exchange, three simple devices were used to make the exchange flow better:

- The use of "and" in Step 3 not only signals that the next question is about to be asked, but also serves to implicitly signal successful receipt of the previous piece of information (age).

- The use of "OK" in Step 5 also signals receipt of information: usually "OK" is used to acknowledge receipt of "small bits" of information—that is, information that can be provided in a few words (e.g., an answer to a yes/no question, a city name, etc.).

- The use of "Got it" in Step 7 signals receipt of the telephone number: in situations where the user was asked to provide a long piece of information, the marker used should not only signal receipt of the information but also acknowledge the effort expended by the user to provide that information. Markers such as "Got it. Thanks," "Thank you," and "Great. Thanks!" all work well as markers acknowledging the effort made by the human user.

Announce That the User Is About to Receive Some Information

In exchanges where a series of questions are asked of the user and then some piece of information is provided (e.g., account balance), the voicebot should always explicitly signal that it is about to provide the user with the requested information. Phrases such as, "Here is your balance" or "Your balance is" are not only perceived to be friendlier than coming back with a raw dollar amount but serve as a cue to the user that they should pay close attention to what the voicebot is about to say.

In situations where the information about to be given will require special concentration from the user, the voicebot could use a longer phrase to prepare the user. For instance, "I am about to give you your 12-digit tracking number."

Mark Sequences

Probably the most jarring aspect of the first example in the previous exchange is the complete lack of any sequencing markers. As mentioned several times in this book, voice-only conversations are both time linear and unidirectional. This means that the voicebot needs to constantly signal to its human counterpart that things are moving forward. Useful markers for achieving this are "and," "now," "next," and "finally."

Mark the Beginning and End of a Section

When an exchange can be structured in larger dialogue block units, marking the beginning and end of a block can greatly help the user position themselves in the problem-solving process and hence prime them to understand what the voicebot expects from them.

The most useful block structuring markers are "Let's start," to mark the beginning of a block, "Next" and "Now," to mark transitions from one block to the next, and explicit statements such as "We are done with the first phase" or "Great! I now have your account information," to mark the end of a block.

In the previous exchange, "First..." in Step 1 and "...I have what I need. I am now setting up your account" in Step 7 signal, respectively, the beginning and the end of the sequence.

It is important to note that marking a sequence of questions is not the same as marking a sequence of larger blocks of dialogue. For example, in a survey of rapid-fire questions, the use of "first," "second," and "third," is appropriate and helps the user keep track of where they are in the flow of questions. But such markers are usually not appropriate for block sequence marking since the time gap between the beginning of one block and the next block is much longer than the one between the beginning of a question and one that follows it. Instead, use markers such as "Next" and "Now," in conjunction with an explicit description of what the upcoming block is about.

Mark Failures

Mark no-inputs, no-matches, and other failures with expressions such as "Sorry, I couldn't hear you" or "Hmm, I didn't get that." A particularly important failure to mark is bad recognition, such as when the voicebot echoes back a piece of information or asks for a confirmation, and the user signals that the voicebot has not recognized them correctly. A brief marker acknowledging that the voicebot has made a mistake makes for a much smoother flow than an abrupt re-asking of the original question:

VOICEBOT: What's your home phone number?

USER: 703-555-1234.

VOICEBOT: That's 703-555-1232. Did I get it right?

USER: No.

VOICEBOT: Sorry about that. Let's try again. Please give me the number one digit at a time.

USER: 703-555-1234.

That said, keep two things in mind: (1) do not dwell too long on apologizing about failures, and (2) make sure the voicebot provides enough information to the user to help them respond in a way that the voicebot will be able to understand.

Show Light at the End of the Tunnel

In dialogues where the user is taxed with a prolonged exchange (e.g., a long survey), use milestone markers to show the user that there is light at the end of the tunnel. Markers such as "We are halfway through," "We are almost done," and "Almost done" are useful to help keep the human energized enough to complete the dialogue.

Indicate Implicitly That the Voicebot Still Owns the Turn

Make sure you never allow your voicebot to go silent for more than 2 or 3 seconds when it owns the conversational turn (i.e., when the voicebot, and not the user, is expected to say something). When a voicebot goes silent, the user usually interprets it as a sign that the voicebot expects them to say something, or worse, that the voicebot has malfunctioned. Dialogue markers such as "One moment please" or "Please hold," followed by a percolating sound are usually effective enough to reassure the user that the voicebot is still active and in possession of the turn.

Tell the User Explicitly That They Are Being Placed on Hold

In situations where you expect the voicebot to take more than 5 seconds to do something, use markers that explicitly tell the user that the wait may be long, such as "Hang on, this may take a few seconds." If the wait is indeed just for a few seconds, a percolation sound is good enough. If the expected wait is 30 seconds or more, on-hold music is more appropriate to indicate that the voicebot is engaged in a task that will take time to complete, but that it still owns the turn.

Don't Repeat the Same Marker Twice in a Row

Note in the following exchange how the second "and" makes the exchange sound a bit jarring without the "OK" stated first (as in Step 5 of the first example in this chapter). Be sure to always take care to read the flow of exchanges to make sure that such repetitive markings do not exist:

> VOICEBOT: First, how old are you?
>
> USER: Twenty-four.
>
> VOICEBOT: And are you male or female?
>
> USER: Female.
>
> VOICEBOT: And what is your home phone number?
>
> USER: 703-555-1234.
>
> VOICEBOT: Got it. Thanks.

Pay Attention to the Markers After a Failure Strategy

Failures are bad not only because they are failures but also because they break the rhythm and flow of a dialogue. Since markers are all about rhythm and flow, make sure you always consider the different failure paths. A dialogue marker that works well when things are moving along smoothly may amplify the jarring feeling caused by a failure if the voicebot designer is not careful.

The following exchange illustrates what happens when you don't pay attention to how a failure strategy clashes with a marker designed to facilitate smoother flow. The clash, in fact, results in an even more jarring piece of dialogue than if the marker had not been inserted in the first place:

> VOICEBOT: How old are you?
>
> USER: Twenty-four.
>
> VOICEBOT: OK. Male or female?
>
> USER: [*silence*].
>
> VOICEBOT: Sorry, I couldn't hear you. OK. Male or female?

CHAPTER 16

Nonverbal Dialogue Marking

A technique that can help the designer compound the added benefits of voice and achieve even higher user satisfaction is the use of nonverbal audio: sounds such as beeps, blips, chimes, and music. Such markers, when deployed judiciously by the designer, can unobtrusively and gently cue the user to do the right thing at the right time, and even add some "audio color" to the user's experience. Such audio serves to punctuate inter-actions, mentally position users in the dialogue, and efficiently establish quick associations between sound and function that would otherwise be cumbersome to communicate with explicit, spoken articulations.

Types of Nonverbal Audio

There are five basic types of nonverbal audio, each useful only for certain dialogue contexts and situations:

Beep or blip
> This is a simple sound with a static pitch. It can be the tra-ditional 1-second beep (for instance, the classic one heard after "Leave your message after the beep"), or a shorter half-second variation of that sound.

Chime

A chime is a slightly more complex sound pattern that is usually used to announce blocks, sections, or new contexts, and to mark transitions.

Earcon

Also known as an "auditory icon," the earcon is the audio equivalent of the visual icon and similarly serves to impart to the user a specific meaning when encountered. For instance, the sound of a bat cracking and a crowd cheering could signal the beginning of the baseball scores section in a dialogue.

Audio logo

An audio logo is a short signature jingle or tune, often no more than a few seconds long, that is vividly associated with a brand in the minds of the users.

Music

Music is usually used at the opening of an interaction, as a light background when offering a list of options, or during times when the user is made to wait either for a voicebot response (if the wait is more than a 10 seconds) or for the next available human agent.

When using nonverbal audio, it is crucial to be consistent:

- Use nonverbal audio across the conversation and not just sporadically (for instance, if you are going to use an earcon when signaling that the voicebot has ceded the turn to the human, this earcon should be used throughout the dialogue and not for just some instances).

- Use the same audio for the same situations (for instance, don't change the wait-for-user-input music between two wait instances during a given dialogue).

The following sections show situations where the use of non-verbal marking could improve your voicebot's usability.

Opening the Dialogue

If the service is provided by a company whose brand is associated with an audio logo (an audio chime, jingle, or tune), then use that audio logo to start the conversation. NBC's famous three-note signature is a good example. McDonald's "I'm lovin' it" would be another. The voicebot could start with the audio logo and then begin the dialogue after that, or by speaking the brand's name, then the audio logo, and then the dialogue.

Signaling That It's the User's Turn to Speak

Usually, a short, soft, 250 millisecond beep can be effective in ensuring that the user understands that it is their turn to speak. This is especially useful if the user does not have any visual cues (i.e., cues that they would get while interacting with Siri or Google Assistant on the phone, or Amazon Echo, which communicates with its blue ring light when it is listening).

Signaling That the Voicebot Is Busy Doing Something and Is Holding the Turn

If the user is made to wait a few seconds (10 or less), then use an earcon (for example, the sound of a keyboard clicking). If the user is made to wait more than 10 seconds, then use music.

Waiting for the User to Give an Answer

There are times when the user is asked for information and the user informs the voicebot that they don't have the information handy and need to go fetch it (for instance, their account number). At such times, while the voicebot is waiting for the human being to come back, some music playing would effectively indicate to the user that the voicebot is patiently waiting for them to get back to the dialogue.

After a No-Input

Use a double beep to quickly and subtly signal to the user that the voicebot did not successfully capture user input and that they wish them to speak again. This is especially useful when the voicebot is interacting with a frequent user of the voicebot who does not need lengthy explanations.

Announcing a List of Choices

Use a chime followed by a verbal landmark, such as "Here's how I can help," before presenting the user with a list of options to pick from.

Entering a New Section

Use an earcon that captures the theme of the new section—as in the sound of the famous New York Stock Exchange bell signaling that the voicebot is about to start engaging the user about stocks, a few seconds of jazz music to signal that the user is entering the entertainment section, and so forth.

Marking Transition from One List Item to the Next

For instance, if you are listing word-definition pairs, one after the next, end each of the pairs with an earcon. The demarcations will impart a sense of order and structure that will enable the user to relax and listen to the content rather than try to figure out if what they are listening to is a new item or part of the previous item.

Announcing Help

Use a chime followed by a verbal landmark, such as "Here's how I can help you."

Ending the Conversation

Fading, tension-releasing, music is usually the best sound for ending a conversation.

CHAPTER 17

Language Design

Let us reiterate our core driving design principle that we have been advocating throughout this book: voicebots are *not* human and, therefore, the humans who will be interacting with these voicebots should *not* be forced, tricked, or even "encouraged" to speak to these voicebots as if they, the voicebots, were human. We saw in Chapter 11 how this principle informs the types of prompts to craft—that is, what the voicebot should say. In this chapter, we touch on the other side of the equation: what language we should expect, and *want*, the user to speak in order to deliver an effective voicebot.

On "Naturalness"

The notion that the user should speak "naturally," as we have previously noted, commits a basic essentialist double error. First, it assumes that there is indeed one way of speaking that is "natural," while other ways are "unnatural"; and second, that this "natural" way is in some sense superior to the "unnatural" ways—and all of this naturalness exists *and is easily accessible at all times in all circumstances*. But in reality, we speak differently when we are addressing, for example, a close friend, a colleague in a professional setting in normal times, a colleague in a professional setting in a time of crisis, a child, our boss, a person who is hard of hearing, or someone who is not fluent in our language. Moreover, we also don't expect the people we speak with to all speak back to us in that purported "natural" way of speaking. Instead, we modulate both what we say and what we expect to hear. If, for instance, we are speaking to someone who is only starting to learn how to speak English, then we are probably not going to expect them to use rare terms, nuanced phrasings, or subtle puns, and we will think we have misheard them if we think they said something that only someone fluent in the language and the culture would say. Similarly, we don't expect our colleagues or our bosses to speak with us in a familiar tone, the way we expect our friends to speak to us, and we would be surprised if they did. In other words, what we listen for is as much a function of our immediate conversational context as what we say is.

So, then, how does the designer build a voicebot that understands what the user says to it?

Key Terms

First, a bit of terminology. We call a representation of the language that the voicebot listens for and responds to a *language model*. This representation could be simply an enumeration of all valid utterances, or it could be some other representation (for instance, grammar rules) that is more compact. As the designer of the voicebot, your task is to come up with this language model.

When a user speaks something that the software is able to process—in other words, when the user speaks something that is in the designed language model—then we say that the user's utterance is *in scope*.

We will call the representation that the software returns to denote the "meaning" of what the user said a *meaning structure*.

Designing an Effective Language Model

To design an effective language model, the first thing you need to do is to control as precisely as possible the framing with which the human enters their conversation with the voicebot. If the user barely knows, or does not know at all, why the voicebot exists or what problems it was designed to solve, then the battle is effectively lost from the start. And it is lost not only because we would be asking too much of a user to learn what they can and cannot say to a voicebot in the heat of a live conversation with that voicebot but, more importantly, because the user enters into the conversation with no clear agenda or goals, and therefore is not motivated to do any work to make things work—to figure out what to say or do.

If you want the human user of your voicebot to know what to say, you need to make sure they come to your voicebot with clear expectations about why the voicebot exists and what problems the user can be helped with. If the user enters in a conversation with a voicebot knowing full well that this is a voicebot that can help them with their water bill, for instance, then chances of success will be high. Why? Simply because the human user will enter the conversation with both the right ontology as well as a goal, and as a result, will come to the conversation ready and motivated to say the right things. The conversation that the human will have with the voicebot will be about the water bill—about deadlines, payments, and the status of the customer's account. With this knowledge, as the designer of the voicebot, you can methodically undertake the task of designing the language—what the user can say, and in fact, will effortlessly say.

So, it is crucial to understand that the task at hand—designing the language that the human will use when engaging with the voicebot—is primarily an *extra-linguistic* one: it has to do first with framing expectations, which in turn will shape an ontology, which, as a third order effect, will result in a language that will be used to manipulate that ontology.

Concretely, in terms of what you as the designer should do, the following three sections show the basic steps you must take if you want to build a language model that your voicebot will understand.

Clearly Define the Problems That Your Voicebot Can Help the User With

Make sure that the reason why the voicebot exists and what problems it can help the user with are easy to grasp by the user and that they form a coherent whole. A good voicebot definition would be: "This voicebot will give you information about your water bill and your account as well as enable you to make credit card payments." A not-so-good voicebot definition would be: "This voicebot is your kitchen mate." The first one talks about actions that refer to a coherent, well-defined set of objects that relate to an overarching goal: giving you "information about your water bill and your account" and enabling you to "make credit card payments." The second one, in contrast, does not. It simply says that the voicebot is your "kitchen mate." But in what way is it a mate? Does it give you advice about what to cook? Does it help you with nutrition information about the food you are cooking? Is it something else? We can't tell. A good kitchen voicebot definition would be: "This voicebot will give you suggestions on what to cook for dinner" or "This voicebot will tell you what essential minerals can be found in any given legume or vegetable." With these two clear and simple-to-understand definitions, the user will know exactly what to say and therefore the designer is able to easily model what the user will say.

Communicate Why the Voicebot Exists and What It Can Help the User Do Outside of the Voicebot

Do not rely on the voicebot to teach the user about the voicebot or to train the user about what it can do. The user should be learning about the purpose of the voicebot somewhere else—on a web page, in a video explainer, in a mobile app—and not when engaged with the voicebot. In our examples of the "kitchen mate" above, if all they know is that this is a voicebot to use in the kitchen, then you can be sure the user is likely to become frustrated very soon after they engage the voicebot. If, on the other hand, the user sees on a website about nutrition a call to action for the user to use a voicebot while in the kitchen—to easily ask about what minerals any vegetable or legume contains—the user will engage that voicebot with clear expectations. Not only will they know what to ask, but they will also engage the voicebot with a purpose, so that even if the voicebot fails to understand a user's language formulation, the user will put in the effort to reformulate their request. They want to know what minerals asparagus has and, knowing that the voicebot can give it to them, they are willing to do what it takes to get that information out of the voicebot.

Spend Time Building a Clean Ontology

Having pinned down why the voicebot exists and what problems it can help with and having determined what to communicate to the user before they use the voicebot (why the voicebot exists and what problems it will help them with), the next step is to build the ontology that the user will enter the conversation with, having been explicitly primed for that ontology.

The user will come with a model of objects (account, current bill, payments, etc.), and those objects will have attributes (account balance, amount due for the current bill, deadline for paying the current bill, latest payment, etc.) and a set of associated actions that the user can take (ask for the balance due, ask about deadlines, pay bills, etc.). Make sure your ontology reflects the ontology the user will have in mind when they engage the voicebot and not some other ontology, such as the one used by the software architects and developers, who may have mapped the world behind the scenes (database tables, functions inside the code) in a completely different way for optimal performance.

Only with this ontology in hand should the creation of the language that the voicebot will listen for begin. The good news is this: no matter what ontology you build, the meaning of every valid thing that the user says can be expressed as a collection of name-value pairs. In the parlance of natural language, the *name* in *name-value* is called *intent*, and *value* is called *slot*. For instance, the question "What is my balance?" can be expressed with a simple intent mapping (e.g., "ask-for-balance"). The statement, "I want to pay 75 dollars" could be represented by the intent "pay-balance" and the slot ("balance-payment-amount," 75 dollars).

Aside from ensuring that you build the right ontology and prime the user with the right framing—so that when they engage the voicebot, they and the voicebot are both navigating the same landscape of objects and functions—here are two additional practical tips on ensuring that the language itself is optimized for robust recognition.

Do Not Design Your Language from the Armchair

Do not make the mistake of thinking that you, in your capacity as a fluent speaker of your natural language (e.g., English), can design the right language model for a water services voicebot. As a fluent speaker of your natural language, you are certainly well equipped to engage with your Voice UX researcher and asking them to tell you the language people use when they are seeking help from a voicebot with their water system. You are also well equipped to design Wizard of Oz sessions with beta users to home in on the language. But at no point are you justified in merely typing up, ex nihilo, examples of what people will say when they engage a voicebot. The temptation will be hard to resist typing what the user is likely to say, but resist that temptation. Don't take the easy way out. Insist on building the language through research and make sure that you engage your UX researcher (or, if you are assuming that responsibility, take off your hat as a designer and earnestly go and do some research). It is this type of principled commitment to grounding what you do on hard-earned evidence and not easy speculation that will turn you into a professional designer.

Go Explicit When Recovering from a Language Error

When a user speaks an out-of-scope utterance, one of these two scenarios is true: (1) they are saying something that is not reasonable to expect from a human being (the user asks about a recipe for making chocolate mousse when talking with a banking voicebot), or (2) they said something reasonable that should be within scope, but the language model did not include it. Either way, when the voicebot reacts to the failure, the voicebot should repeat its request, but this time being explicit about what the user should say:

> USER: I want to know how much I owe you.
>
> VOICEBOT: Sorry, I didn't understand. You can say, "Check my balance," "Pay my bill," or "Something else."
>
> USER: Check my balance.

CHAPTER 18

On Silence

Silence for VUI design is what the number zero is for algebra. As a concept and a tool, it is at the same time essential, ubiquitous, and taken for granted.

In this chapter, we highlight the main cases where the use of silences and pauses can contribute to a smoother, more usable voice user experience.

Here's a brief interaction between a stock management voicebot and a human user:

> VOICEBOT: Here's what you can do: get quotes, buy stock, or sell stock. You can also say, "Speak to a manager."
>
> USER: Get quotes.
>
> VOICEBOT: Getting quotes. As of 10:25 a.m., IBM is trading at eighty-two dollars and thirty-five cents, Apple at one hundred three dollars and twenty-four cents, and Google at three hundred seventy-four dollars and thirteen cents.

Let's pinpoint where silences can enhance the usability of the user's experience.

Prior to Listing Options

When the voicebot is about to provide the user with a list of options, a brief, half-second pause should be inserted between the announcement prompt and the first option that is played to the listener:

> VOICEBOT: Here's what you can do:
>
> [*silence*]
>
> get quotes, buy stock, or sell stock. You can also say,
>
> [*silence*]
>
> "Speak to a manager."

Be careful with the language that precedes the enumeration of the options lest the language triggers the user to speak too soon. For instance, if the voicebot were to say, "What can I help you with?" and then pause, the user may start speaking, since that is a full request in its own right. In contrast, "Here's what you can do" is an announcement that signals to the user that the voicebot is about to provide them with additional information.

Between Options in a Menu List

When listing options for the user to select from, separate consecutive options with 200 millisecond silences. The pauses will give the listener time to decide whether to select the option or wait for the next option:

> VOICEBOT: Here's what you can do:
>
> [*silence*]
>
> get quotes,
>
> [*silence*]
>
> buy stock, or

[*silence*]

sell stock. You can also say,

[*silence*]

"Speak to a manager."

Between Categories of Options

In our example, the voicebot plays to the user three possible stock-related commands to choose from, and then plays one more option for transferring to a manager. Since the fourth option is not a stock-related command, a pause between 500 milliseconds and 1 second should be inserted between the last stock command option and the announcement for the next command, "You can also say…":

VOICEBOT: Here's what you can do:

[*silence*]

get quotes,

[*silence*]

buy stock, or

[*silence*]

sell stock.

[*silence*]

You can also say,

[*silence*]

"Speak to a manager."

When Interacting with Power Users

Most of the users of the stock voicebot we are using for this example are going to be repeat users—that is, power users who will not want to listen to all the menu options every time they call. With such heavy power-user voicebots, use longer silences prior to listing menu options. In this case, for instance, you can add a pause up to 2 seconds after "Here's what you can do":

VOICEBOT: Here's what you can do:

[*silence*]

get quotes,

[*silence*]

buy stock, or

[*silence*]

sell stock.

[*silence*]

You can also say,

[*silence*]

"Speak to a manager."

After Echoing

A brief echo from the voicebot of the option selected by the user can serve as a reassuring confirmation that the voicebot understood what the user said, or, in case of misrecognition, as a quick indication of error. In either case, insert a brief silence after the echo. In case of correct recognition, the silence will prepare the user for the next prompt, while in case of misrecognition, it will give the user an opportunity to barge in with a correction. Of course, you will need to configure an error strategy that can elegantly recover from such an error:

VOICEBOT: Here's what you can do:

[*silence*]

get quotes,

[*silence*]

buy stock, or

[*silence*]

sell stock.

[*silence*]

You can also say,

[*silence*]

"Speak to a manager."

USER: Get quotes.

VOICEBOT: Getting quotes.

[*silence*]

As of 10:25 a.m....

Before and After TTS Prompts

As we have mentioned in Chapter 11, avoid mixing recorded prompts with computerized TTS prompts. Mixed prompts make for an unpleasant audio experience and should be avoided whenever possible. In cases where you have no choice but to mix human-recorded and computer-generated prompts, insert a pause between the recorded prompts and the TTS prompts. The silence will alleviate the jarring transition and will increase the level of listener comprehension:

VOICEBOT: Getting quotes.

[*silence*]

As of 10:25 a.m.,

[*silence*]

IBM is trading at

[*silence*]

eighty-two dollars and thirty-five cents,

[*silence*]

Apple at

[*silence*]

one hundred three dollars and twenty-four cents,

[*silence*]

and Google at

[*silence*]

three hundred seventy-four dollars and thirteen cents.

Here is the entire interaction, with all silences inserted:

VOICEBOT: Here's what you can do:

[*silence*]

get quotes,

[*silence*]

buy stock, or

[*silence*]

sell stock.

[*silence*]

You can also say,

[*silence*]

"Speak to a manager."

USER: Get quotes.

VOICEBOT: Getting quotes.

[*silence*]

As of 10:25 a.m.,

[*silence*]

IBM is trading at

[*silence*]

eighty-two dollars and thirty-five cents,

[*silence*]

Apple at

[*silence*]

one hundred three dollars and twenty-four cents,

[*silence*]

and Google at

[*silence*]

three hundred seventy-four dollars and thirteen cents.

CHAPTER 19

The Elements of Closing

Dialogues with voicebots end in one of five ways:

- The user explicitly stops the dialogue. ("Hey Google, stop.")

- The user implicitly ends the dialogue (they just stopped responding to the voicebot).

- The user requests to be directed to a human. ("I want to talk to someone.")

- The voicebot determines that the user needs to be directed to a human.

- The voicebot determines that the dialogue has reached its end and ends the dialogue. ("This is the end of the survey. Thank you for participating. Goodbye!")

There is little that the voicebot can do in reaction to the first case. For the other scenarios, the following rules should be observed when closing a dialogue.

Allow the Users to Explicitly End the Dialogue

In a context where a valid user option is for the user to simply abandon the dialogue (e.g., quitting after successfully executing a transfer and are back to the main list of options), let the user know that they can say, "Quit" or "Goodbye," or that they can simply hang up in the case of a phone call. Users may find it unnatural (or impolite) to end a dialogue by simply hanging up, so telling them that it's perfectly OK to do so would alleviate that natural hang-up (no pun intended):

> VOICEBOT: Here's what you can do: check your balance, withdraw funds, or transfer funds. If you are done, say "Goodbye" or just hang up.

Allow the User to Request a Human

If connecting the user to a human is an available option, you should let users know that this is indeed an option. And not only when they are having trouble using the voicebot, but from the very start. Users appreciate not feeling forced to engage with the voicebot and they may engage with it more cooperatively if they know they have a choice.

When the User Has to Wait, Provide a Waiting Time Estimate

In cases where the voicebot has the option of transferring the user to a human, or if they are promised that a human will get back to them, provide the user with an estimate of the time the user will need to wait prior to talking to a human, if possible.

Provide the Option to Cancel a Transfer to a Human

After providing the user with an estimate of how long it will take to reach a human, provide the user with the option of canceling the transfer and returning to the voicebot dialogue. The human may change their mind after hearing that the wait time is longer than they expected and may decide to work with the voicebot in those cases where the human asked for a human as soon as the dialogue started.

Keep the "While-You-Wait" Audio Relevant

Users hate to be placed on hold. But what they hate more is being forced to listen to marketing pitches that are not relevant to their needs while they are waiting. If you are playing something other than music, make sure the audio you play while the user is waiting is relevant to the user and is focused on helping the user solve the problem they engage the voicebot about—or at the least useful in some way to the user (e.g., information about potential discounts, upcoming events). For instance, if the user has a dangerously low checking balance and the voicebot determines that they are in danger of bouncing checks, the voicebot can suggest that the user requests information about the overdraft protection plan from the human.

Understand the User's State of Mind When You Play the "While-You-Wait" Audio

Make sure your voicebot is sensitive to the emotional state of the user. If the user is likely to be frustrated or anxious (for instance, they are opening a new ticket or want to get the latest status of a ticket they opened), having the voicebot boast about how the company had just won an industry award is likely to irritate the user.

Never Say, "Your Call Is Important to Us"

Another overused phrase that should be retired.

Don't Make the User Repeat to the Human Information They Provided to the Voicebot

One of the biggest complaints that users have about voicebots is the notorious practice of forcing users to repeat to humans information they had just provided to the voicebot. There are three ways to address this failure in usability:

- Pass to the human whatever information was collected— whether by a screen pop[1] or an audio whisper to the human prior to connecting.

- If the voicebot can't pass information to the human, then, if possible, have the human ask for information different from what the voicebot requested from the user; for instance, if the voicebot asked the user for their account ID, the human should ask the user for, say, their phone number, and with that, try to look up the user's account ID. The goal is to avoid, whenever possible, making the user repeat themselves.

- At least, have the human apologize for making the user repeat themselves, and have the human ask only for the minimum to accomplish their task.

---

1 *Computer telephony integration* (CTI) is the technology that enables the displaying of information collected about the customer to the person receiving the call.

Make the Human Agent Aware That the Customer Was Interacting with the Voicebot

In cases where no information is being passed from the voicebot to the human, at the very least, make sure the human agent is alerted that the user they are speaking with was just interacting with a voicebot. The agent can then adjust their behavior accordingly (e.g., sympathize with the user if they know that users transferred from the voicebot are usually frustrated).

Avoid Transferring Users from One Voicebot to Another

Unless the voicebots are designed as units of a common whole (with identical voices and with information collected from the first voicebot passed along to the second, etc.), don't transfer users from one voicebot to another voicebot.

Don't Play Phone Rings Unless You Are Transferring Directly to a Human

The sound of a phone ringing after an interaction with a voicebot is a signal to the user that they are about to speak to a human. Don't play phone rings and then present the user with yet another voicebot.

Reassure Users of Success

If the main purpose of an interaction was to execute a transaction and the transaction was successfully completed, inform the user that the transaction was successful and, if possible, let them know that a follow-up confirmation will reach them. Ideally, an email or a text message detailing the transaction should be sent. Such a communication will serve as a reassuring, persistent, visible, warm-and-fuzzy action, and will go a long way toward reducing the number of inquiries (e.g., calls or emails into the contact center) from people who just want to make sure the voicebot did what it was supposed to do:

> VOICEBOT: Great! We are done! You should receive an email shortly detailing your transaction.

Don't Provide Any Crucial New Information

Whether the call termination was initiated by the user or the voicebot, try to avoid announcing anything new or important at the interaction-closing prompt. After the user says, "Goodbye," their attention to what the voicebot is saying is minimal. At most, repeat some piece of information before closing with "Goodbye," for example, "And please remember, once again, your coupon is valid only through June 30th. Goodbye."

Give the User a Quick Tip

If the user had to traverse a complex flow to reach the option they selected, whenever possible the voicebot should tip the user on how, next time they engage with it, they can make their selection with an easy-to-remember shortcut:

> USER: Goodbye.

> VOICEBOT: Great. For next time, remember that if you just need a quick summary of your account, just say, "Account summary." Thanks again. Bye!

Note, however, that the tip needs to be provided quickly, at the very beginning of the closing sequence before the user stops listening.

Offer to Reach Back

If the voicebot determines that the user needs to wait three minutes or more to speak with a human, then offer the user the option to be reached back (via a notification, a text, or a callback) by the voicebot when a human is available to speak with the user.

CHAPTER 20

Voice First Notifications

When we think of a human assistant, we usually think of someone who is at our beck and call, available to help us with our requests, and who tries their best to fulfill such requests. But a good assistant does not just wait for our request and then react. A good assistant is proactive and takes initiative, and because they are familiar with our schedules, our preferences, goals, and values, they can often *anticipate* not only what we may want to do, but also when and how we want to do it. And if they are really good at what they do, they also know what we want to avoid doing and why.

For example, a conscientious human assistant will make sure we receive information that comes to their attention and they feel we may need to be aware of. But a great assistant will also know which information is urgent and needs to be brought to our attention immediately, which information can wait until the next time they interact with us, which information can wait just for the right time, and which information not to bother us with.

If we want to build a voicebot that acts similarly—for instance, a voicebot that monitors our email, inbound SMS (short message service) texts, instant message chats, and calendar, to enable us to focus on our work (say, we have carved out two hours to focus on writing a book), but at the same time not miss important things (for instance, meetings, urgent email from clients, a chat message from an employee who is blocked by you)—we need to design the voicebot carefully so that it doesn't make costly mistakes (for example, needlessly interrupting us with notifications that could have waited or failing to deliver important messages in a timely fashion).

In this chapter, we touch on some fundamental considerations and key dimensions when thinking through the design of voicebot notification features.

Fundamental Considerations

Three fundamental considerations need to be kept in mind if you want your voicebot to deliver great proactive notification experiences:

- Notifications, by their definition, are events—and events are time creatures in that they have a starting time and an ending time.

- Because time is linear, a notification *will* interrupt a flow of events—or several flows of events at the same time if the notification is delivered to several people at the same time or if the user receiving the notification is multitasking.

- Notifications deliver two pieces of information: (1) the fact of the existence of a notification, and (2) the content of the notification itself. For instance, a sound or a yellow flashing light alerts us that a message has arrived, while the message itself that has arrived is the content of the notification.

Key Notification Attributes

To determine how to deliver a notification, the following attributes need to be kept in mind.

Notification Urgency

- How urgent is it for the user to receive the notification? Can the notification wait or does it need to be delivered now? There are many reasons a user may want to be notified immediately. For instance, the user may want to know that an important trouble ticket they opened with a vendor is being taken care of, or that the car is ready to pick up from the shop. Such notifications may not only help them relax more but may help them schedule the rest of their day accordingly (I don't need to call the vendor again, as I had planned to, and since the car is ready one day earlier, I will pick it up and not catch a ride back home with one of my colleagues).

- How urgent is it for the user to quickly act on the notification? Is there a cost to the user if they don't act on the notification in a timely fashion? A notification that it is time to reorder paper for the printer is less urgent to act on *now* than a notification that the user left the garage door open as they drove away.

Notification Content

- How sensitive is the information that is being shared? Personal information relating to health, finances, and family matters needs to be treated differently than general news or work-related matters.

- How complex is the information and would it make sense to render it by voice? Short messages such as "Your car is ready" are perfect for voice notifications, but the content of a trouble ticket, spanning several paragraphs, would not be.

Delivery Context

- What is the user's physical context? Are they likely to be awake or asleep, at home or in the office? Are they in a noisy environment where it may be hard for them to hear the information spoken to them by the voicebot?

- What is the user's social context? Are they alone or are they with other people? Are those people family members, friends, colleagues, or strangers?

- Has this notification been sent to the user before? Are they likely to have heard it already?

- What is the track record of the user with prior notifications? Do they listen to them or ignore them? They see a flashing light on the smart speaker indicating that a notification has arrived and is ready for them to listen to it. Do they ask to listen to it or just ignore it?

- How about acting on the content of the notifications: do they listen to them and then do nothing, or do they act on them (e.g., they reorder the paper when they hear a notification that tells them they are running out of paper)?

Key Form Factors

How a voicebot should act when faced with the decision of what to do depends not only on the above considerations but also on the form factor mediating the voicebot's interaction with the human. How (or even whether) the notification will be delivered will depend on whether the receiving device is a smart speaker, a smartphone, a landline, or an earbud.

Far-Field Voice

By its very nature, far-field voice is a one-to-many medium: the voicebot is broadcasting audio that can be heard by more than one person at the same time. This is perfectly fine in, say, a family home setting where the voicebot is answering a question about the weather, but not fine when they are at work and the information that is being broadcast is personal (lab results or bank balance, for instance).

Near-Field Voice

Unlike far-field voice, near-field voice is almost always a one-to-one experience. Usually, near-field voice is delivered on a smartphone or a tablet to the owner of that device, and it is up to that user to put it in speaker mode, control the volume so that they are the only who can hear it, or put it against their ear to ensure that no one else but themselves can hear it.

In-Ear Voice

Here, we have a truly one-to-one experience (unless the user is sharing their earbuds with someone else), hence a greater assurance of privacy—assuming that the targeted user is the one who is wearing the device.

Some Best Practices

We've provided some best practices for handling notifications.

Be Mindful of the Receiver's Time Zone

Don't assume that all notification receivers are in the same time zone. If you have access to the time zone of the recipients, take that into consideration. In cases where the message is not urgent and does not need to be heard immediately, adjust the timing so that it is not received in off-hours. Sending a notification at 10:00 a.m. to everyone means that those on the West Coast will receive it at 7:00 a.m., which is not ideal, especially given that the notification will make noise and probably wake up some people.

Provide Some Context

A notification is almost by definition a message that's coming in out of the blue. Make sure you include in the notification information who the sender is and why the notice is being sent.

Instead of:

> VOICEBOT: Hello. This is to let you know that the weekly newsletter has been sent out! Enjoy!

Use:

> VOICEBOT: Hello from Sonic Sunday! This is a quick heads-up to let you know that the newsletter is now out! Enjoy!

Cut to the Chase

Instead of:

> VOICEBOT: Hello from Sonic Sunday! I hope you are enjoying your weekend so far. This is a quick heads-up to let you know that the newsletter is now out!

Use:

> VOICEBOT: Hello from Sonic Sunday! This is a quick heads-up to let you know that the newsletter is now out! Enjoy the rest of your weekend.

Repeat the Important Information

Instead of:

> VOICEBOT: Hello from Longfellow Middle School! This is to let you know that, due to snow, all Fairfax county schools will be starting two hours late today.

Use:

> VOICEBOT: Hello from Longfellow Middle School! This is to let you know that, due to snow, all Fairfax county schools will be two hours late today. Repeat:

Due to snow, all Fairfax county schools will be starting two hours late today.

Provide the User with a Way to Get More Details

In cases where you know that the notification sent will trigger users to seek additional information, include in the notification some guidance on how to receive such information.

Use:

> VOICEBOT: Hello from Longfellow Middle School! This is to let you know that, due to snow, all Fairfax county schools will be starting two hours late today. Repeat: Due to snow, all Fairfax county schools will be starting two hours late today. To find out more, go to: www.fcps.edu. That's www.fcps.edu.

Some Scenarios

The above considerations, characteristics, and form factors should enable the designer to take any notification scenario and carefully think through how to design voicebot notification strategies that align with the use cases it encounters.

Obviously, to successfully execute on such strategies, the voicebot needs to have access to the information it needs. Some of that information may be easy to obtain (e.g., the form factor is a smart speaker or a smartphone), other information it might be able to collect (e.g., the user's track record when it comes to answering or acting on notifications), and yet other information may be difficult to obtain directly but could be inferred (e.g., whether the user is in a quiet or noisy environment given the frequency of out-of-scope error occurrence).

Following are a few scenarios to illustrate the kind of thinking the designer should be doing.

Scenario 1

The voicebot is planning to send a notification deemed by the voicebot to be both urgent and sensitive. The only form factor available to the voicebot is a smart speaker. What specific design considerations come into play?

First, given that the notification is deemed urgent, the voicebot should not only send that notification as soon as possible but should also ensure that it sends it again if the user doesn't act on it. Second, given that the information the notification is delivering is deemed sensitive, when the voicebot is interacting with the user it needs to discreetly let the user know that the information is sensitive and should ask for their permission to speak it before giving such information out loud. If the user declines to hear the information, the urgent information should be made available to the user through some other means (for instance, via email) and the user should be told that an important email has been sent that requires the user's immediate attention.

Scenario 2

The voicebot is planning to send a notification deemed by the voicebot not to be urgent, and it is late at night. The form factors available to the voicebot are the smartphone and the earbuds. What does the voicebot do?

Obviously, the voicebot should schedule the notification for the next morning, during working hours.

Scenario 3

The voicebot is planning to send a notification deemed by the voicebot to be urgent but not sensitive. The devices available to the voicebot are a smart speaker, a smartphone, and earbuds.

In this case, the voicebot should send a notification to all the user's devices and speak the content of the notification without the cautionary warning it would use with sensitive content.

CHAPTER 21

Laying Out the Foundations

Far too often, voicebots are conceived by the businesses that deploy them as little more than a necessary evil. After all, common wisdom goes that users will always prefer to speak to and interact with a human being instead of a machine, so forcing a user to endure an automated assistant is almost by definition viewed as an imposition to the user—especially a user who bothered to reach out to you seeking your business!

But designing voicebots with this "necessary evil" conception in mind almost invariably results in voicebots that are indeed an imposition on those who have to endure them. In cases where the user is expecting to speak with a human—and since the user is going to wince and whine as soon as they realize that they have to speak with a voicebot—the best that can be expected from the voiceobt designer is to mitigate damage and hope for the best.

But more harmful than the mediocre voicebots that such a view of voicebot design and development engender are the missed golden opportunities to turn voicebots into branding assets and marketing opportunities.

In this chapter, we outline what it takes to begin thinking about designing voicebots with the goal of turning an interaction with a voicebot into an opportunity-enablement channel.

Bring Together All the Key Players

Whether you are building a house, a car, or a voicebot, truly intelligent design begins with collecting information from those with the key pieces of knowledge needed to design for a solid end product.

In the case of designing a voicebot that will truly serve both user needs and positively impact business goals, both short-term and long-term, the following players must be consulted early and often:

Contact center agents
> Their role is to ground the design and the discussion in "the real world" and to share their workaday insights about user needs, goals, and behavior. Agent input will enable the identification of those tasks that agents would gladly like to see off-loaded, and hence positioning the voicebot as a helper of the agents rather than a threatening competitor.

Customer service managers
> Their role is to serve as vocal advocates for customer needs.

Business decision makers
> They will identify the immediate business goals they want the voicebot to accomplish for their company and will spell out the company's broader business strategy. What can the voicebot help with most effectively? Detecting potential churn, ensuring that new customers are onboarded smoothly, getting old customers back, and upselling current customers? Yes, the voicebot can help with all of the above, but perhaps there is one specific problem or opportunity that the voicebot can help with most effectively—given the nature of the business, the nature of the product or service the customer is buying, or what the biggest problem that the business is trying to focus on solving now.

The marketing team
> Their role is to ensure that the company's brand is respected and promoted through the voicebot, that the voicebot, where appropriate, is amplifying the company's messaging and is aligned with other channels (social media, mobile, website, etc.).

The development team
> This consists not only of engineers but more crucially of *UX researchers*, *UX designers*, and *product managers*. Their role is to listen carefully to the stakeholders, ask questions, and fully understand the business context within which they are building.

Define the Business Goals

Voicebot design cannot begin without first clearly establishing the business goals that are expected to be met through the deployment of the voicebot.

Here are a few examples of business goals:

- Cutting down on the number of calls handled by live agents by off-loading to the voicebot those tasks that naturally lend themselves to self-service (e.g., checking balance, reviewing the most recent credit card transactions).

- Cutting down on the amount of time live agents spend with customers.

- Qualifying calls prior to transferring to live agents.

- Improving customer satisfaction; for instance, enabling users to execute a self-service transaction (e.g., obtain their account balance or the status of their ordered service) rather than wait idly for the next available agent.

- Increasing revenue: taking advantage of up-selling or cross-selling opportunities that may present themselves.

- Increasing retention rates: proactively identifying problems and moving to resolve them; identifying lost clients and moving to win them back.

Define User Needs and Intent

The third pillar to building a solid voicebot is your knowledge of users: who are they, what do they say they need, and what do they really want? Build a profile of the user through the following factors:

Emotional state
> If users are likely to be agitated or under some stress (service emergency hotline), a happy voice with a cheerful jingle is probably not the appropriate persona; what is needed is a serious, low-key voice that echoes the sense of urgency the user is experiencing.

Age
> What is the age distribution of the users? Knowledge about user age could influence, among other things, design of prompt verbiage, the speech rate to adopt, the amount of time to give users to respond, and the amount of instructions to give users.

Technical savvy
> Are users at ease with voicebots or are they likely to be flustered?

Expertise level
> Are users frequent users of the system or are they one-time users?

Opportunity type
> Is the user a student with a low balance who usually calls to make sure his balance is not dangerously low, or are they a homeowner with a large balance? Such information will help you intelligently design effective up-sell and cross-sell opportunities.

Identify User Tasks

What is the user ostensibly engaging about? Here are some examples of tasks that users could be attempting to accomplish:

- Log a new trouble ticket.
- Check on the status of a trouble ticket.
- Seek account balance.
- Inquire about service status.
- Request a service activation.
- Make a payment.
- Register for an event.

Identify Usage Patterns

Computers are very good at sifting through reams of data and detecting patterns. Instead of treating all users the same way by, for instance, offering them the same menu choices or the same flows, regardless of who is engaging, what if the voicebot could make an informed guess as to what the user is engaging about? Pay attention to the following patterns:

Use patterns

Are there patterns to task requests across time for a given user? What if the voicebot could detect that a certain user engages every Saturday morning to ask for their balance, and then adapt its behavior so that whenever it engages with the user on Saturday mornings, it gives the user their balance right off the bat? Establishing such customer-centric intelligence and then acting on that intelligence is a sure way to build lasting brand loyalty from customers.

Task request patterns

Are there usage patterns that can be exploited to help users fulfill their needs quickly and efficiently? What if on the first Monday of every month, 90% of users engage the voicebot to renew their monthly pass? Why not take advantage of that knowledge and have the assistant ask users upfront if they want to renew their monthly pass? Chances are that the voicebot will get it right 90% of the time!

Task request dependencies
If someone has engaged to log a new trouble ticket, the next time they engage, they will likely ask about the status of that ticket. Your voicebot should be smart in that way.

Define the Voicebot's Voice Register

Spoken language is an intimate communication medium. When we hear a voice, we reflexively associate that voice with a personality. This is why voicebots, whether by design or by accident, always have an emotional voice register; they come across as serious, formal, casual, or fun, whether or not the designer deliberately meant the voicebot to sound so.

What we call *voice register* here is much more than the sound of the voicebot's voice. It also refers to considerations such as the type of language they use (formal or casual; uses idioms or slang or not), their conversation style (do they drive the conversation—the dialogue is directed; or are they tolerant of deviations—the initiative is mixed), and how they phrase their statements and questions ("How old are you?" versus "What is your age?").

By taking control of their voicebot's voice register,[1] the designer can improve the usability of the voicebot by seeking to accomplish two things.

---

1 This is called *persona* in some quarters, but our stand is to avoid talking about personas since a persona evokes a human being and we prefer not to introduce anthropomorphizing tools and concepts. It is better to think directly about the characteristics of the voice than to draw a personality and then lean on it to answer questions.

First, ensure that the register of the voicebot reflects the brand of the business or organization that it represents. Second, ensure that the voicebot's voice register is coherent and consistent throughout its interactions. Should it say, "I didn't get that" or "I didn't understand that"? Should the voice be that of an older gentleman or a younger lady? By having a well-defined voice register clearly in mind, prompt writing becomes easier for the designer.

CHAPTER 22

The Key to Successful Product Launches

You may have heard or read somewhere that Amazon, Google, and Apple, among other companies, all use something called the *working backwards method* when they undertake to launch a product, a project, a program, or anything that requires a team of people to deliver. That is, they start from envisioning clearly the end result and then work backwards from there to figure out where to start and how to move from there to that envisioned end. The method is meant to be both an exercise in creating clarity and a process at the end of which a concrete document is delivered by the document owner—in the case where the deliverable is a product, the product manager—to a team of stakeholders that will serve that team as a guiding, go-to source to answer all questions they may have about the product.

At Amazon, for instance, they use a method called PR/FAQ: (Press Release and Frequently Asked Questions). The PR/FAQ document consists of two sections:

- An actual press release describing in clear, lay terms that anyone can read and understand, focusing on mainly the value but also the key features that enable the delivery of that value.

- A FAQ list, which is a list of questions and answers covering all aspects of the product.

A measure of how successful an initial PR/FAQ is can be measured by comparing the PR/FAQ's press release and the actual press release that was used to launch the product. If the two are very similar, then it means the initial vision was right on target.

For instance, when we set about to write this book, we put together a PR/FAQ and we wrote an actual, fully fleshed-out press release as well as a detailed FAQ.

Doing this made us put the vision of this book in sharp focus. What sort of a book could we write that would be worth reading and that therefore would deserve a press release? This was difficult to do, but it forced us to ask the question, "But, seriously, why does the world need another voice user interface design book?"

Once we pinned down the press release, we went on to ask ourselves some other basic tough questions such as "Who is the target reader?" and "Why would they buy our book over one of the other books?" and so on. Once we were done with the PR/FAQ, we had the foundation to write the book and we were motivated: we knew what we were writing in this book, who would read it, why they would benefit from it, and that they would buy it even if they were to have all of the other excellent books that are available today.

In our case, the product that we were putting together was the book. In your case, the product is the voicebot that you want to build.

The following sections give you some tips on how to write a powerful PR/FAQ that will serve as the backbone to *your* product building.

Write Everything Out in Full Sentences

Use words, and only words, making sure that every single word is part of a full sentence. No matter how tempting, do not use images, videos, audio, charts, or graphs: use only words. This means no bullet points (unless each bullet point is a full sentence). You may use whatever you want in appendices that contain supplementary material to the PR/FAQ, but every single question in your FAQ needs to have an answer that completely answers the question in words only. And push yourself to write in narrative style and not in bulleted items. Why? Because language that flows with no skips reflects thinking that flows with no skips. Bullet points, in contrast, are dangerous because they may create gaps and elisions. And it is in these gaps and elisions that errors, big or small, dwell.

Your Press Release Needs to Be Crystal Clear

Here's what your press release needs to do:

- It needs to describe the product or the service in terms that the general public can understand: (1) the value that is being delivered to the market, and (2) the features that deliver that value.

- It provides two quotes (they can be made up) that a typical user of the product you are launching may say when interviewed about the product.

- It provides a quote from an executive from the company that is deploying the product or service.

- If there are partners, it should have quotes from them explaining their role.

- It ends with a sentence or two about next steps along with information that is important for the reader to know (for instance, what language the product or service is available in, when the product will be available generally if the announcement is about a limited release, etc.).

Your Answers Are Given in One or Two Paragraphs at Most, and Not Much More

To deliver a potent FAQ, make sure you put in the effort to be as succinct as possible, without being cryptic.

Answer the Basic Questions First

Start by answering the obvious questions: each of the questions being its own paragraph or two:

- What is this?
- Why are we doing it?
- What's the closest thing to what we are doing and how do we differ?
- Why would someone buy what we are building and not the alternatives?
- How large is the market?
- How will we price this?
- If the project succeeds, what would be the main reason it did?
- If the project fails, what would be the main reason it did?
- If you provide clear answers to these questions, you are off to a great start.

Describe Clearly the Research You Have Done

Your PR/FAQ needs to be grounded in reality, so make sure that any claims of fact you make are backed by solid data. Literally, you need a question in the FAQ that asks, "What sources have you used to obtain the data you are using and how reliable are those sources?" If there is research that suggests evidence that may counter any hypothesis you are putting forward, such evidence and the research behind it need to be called out and discussed. The last thing you want to do is suppress information that could easily help you avoid making bad decisions.

Be Modest and Cautious in Your Claims and Statements

Avoid hyperbole at all costs. A good way of doing this is to kill as many adverbs as possible. Your PR/FAQ should not include words such as "extremely," "very," or "greatly." Instead of writing, "We expect customers will find the feature really useful," simply say, "We expect customers will find the feature useful."

In addition to avoiding hyperbole, be self-reflexive and do not pretend to have final answers. The reader needs to feel through your tone that, while you are making the best possible case and that you feel your case is strong, they must also sense that you are open to changing your mind if solid evidence is presented to you.

Make Your Document Readable by Everyone

Readability makes your document accessible to the many perspectives you will need to ensure that when launched, your product will be at the very least minimally viable. A lawyer should be able to pick your PR/FAQ, read it, and understand it from end to end. The same for marketers, the billing folks, the sales team, quality engineers, software developers, investors, partners, the CEO, and members of the customer care team—they should all be able to pick up the document, read it, and understand it from end to end. You want this because you want them to be able to give you feedback from their perspective: a billing person may point out that you have not covered how this new product will be billed, while a lawyer may surface a bad assumption you made that would need to be addressed before any work starts.

To that end—making your document readable: (1) Avoid all jargon; (2) do not assume any expert prior knowledge; and (3) write in short, to-the-point sentences. Your aim is clarity: repetition is just fine if the repetition creates clarity. Explicitly explaining what a pronoun is referring to is just fine if that explanation creates clarity.

List the Functional Requirements in Terms of What the User Can Do

The functional requirements need to be nothing more (and nothing less) than a list of full sentences that all start with "The user is able to…." Do not talk about how something is done; do not talk about the technology behind the scenes. The functional requirements talk only about one thing: the *what*. The *why* should have been addressed in previous questions in the FAQ and the *how* will be addressed later in the detailed design and then after that in the engineering plan.

Describe the Intended Minimum Viable Product (MVP) in Detail

What set of features will you start on initial launch? And what evidence do you have that this set of features is no smaller and no larger than exactly the set you need for launch? You can then determine what additional features need to be added or what adjustments need to be made to your product; hence, the product's viability is substantially enhanced and the product is placed on stable footing and on a path for scalable adoption.

Writing PR/FAQs requires patience, practice, and a lot of hard work. Your first PR/FAQ you will write is going to be painful. You will feel that the requirement to write everything out in full sentences is unreasonable and that it's OK to take shortcuts. Resist that temptation. Writing full sentences is going to force you to write for the larger audience outside of your immediate team. Remember, the PR/FAQ is written to be read by members coming from all the functions of your organization, so resist shorthand. Moreover, writing in full sentences will check your natural impulse to elide your thoughts. But once you get the hang of it—usually after you have written half a dozen such PR/FAQs—you will simply not be able to work without them. And that's a good thing.

CHAPTER 23

The Elements of Deployment

Successfully launching any product, digital or physical, requires a team of several talented professionals, each proficient in their own specialty, working collaboratively toward a common goal, with a common timeline, and enabled by a product manager who does their job just as professionally as any other member of the team: they provide a clear, exciting vision, help plan and organize, and ensure that everyone stays focused by protecting and empowering the members of the team.

In this chapter, we go over the roles that one finds in a typical product team.

Product Management

The product manager, also sometimes referred to as the product owner, is the person to whom the glory goes if the product succeeds, and the shame if the product fails. The buck stops with the product manager.

The very first step that a product manager must take to set the project on a path toward success is to ensure that every single member of the team understands what each other member of that team does and why the role of that member, and therefore the member themself, is important to delivering a high-quality product.

In fact, one of the product manager's primary tasks throughout the delivery of a product is to detect gaps in such understanding. For instance, an engineer may be fuzzy about who is supposed to come up with the functional requirements (that would be the product manager), or a quality engineer may not know who to pull into the conversation when they have feedback about the usability of a feature (that would be the UX designer). It's a product manager's responsibility to bridge those gaps.

The product manager is also the one who must do whatever it takes to ensure that the right team is assembled; the right product is built; the product is priced effectively and built according to the specifications; the specifications are the correct specifications, detailed enough, coherent, and based on real data; and so on.

A product manager is the one who gets upset if a deadline is not met or a requirement is not implemented correctly, and the one who makes sure that resources are available, the scope is reasonable, the details are provided to those who need them, the team members are motivated and understand why they are doing what they are doing—and a million other things. Think of the product manager as the producer of a movie, or even better, as the CEO of a startup.

It is also the product manager's job to ensure that the product is marketed correctly, supported adequately once launched to the market, monitored closely, and delivers to the company's bottom line: whether in terms of revenue, profitability, strategy, branding, or a combination thereof.

You, as the voicebot designer, will need to get very close to the product manager. A good product manager knows a lot and can help you get to the information you need. They have the vision of what needs to be delivered: they understand the user, the business buyer, the problem the product is going to solve for the end user, and the value it will deliver to the business buyer.

It is also important to understand that the strategic management of the team belongs to the product manager: they need to provide the team with a compelling, exciting vision; motivate the team; ensure that resources are available; and advocate on behalf of the end user and the business buyer. But it is equally important to understand that the effective product manager is someone who is in the trenches with their team. Their role is not to micromanage them or to "supervise" them but to be there when they have a question or concern, a creative block, or when they are upset because someone they depended on to meet their deadline failed them. The effective product manager is always busy planning, teaching, learning, putting out fires, helping, motivating, and keeping everyone's eyes, including theirs, on the ball.

Aside from strategic planning and tactical intervention, the most important key deliverable that the product manager owns is the product's set of functional requirements—what the user will be able to do using the product. The document that details these requirements is a foundational document, and the success or the failure of the product will hinge on it. If the product manager gets the functional requirements wrong, no matter how well-designed the product is, how well that design is implemented by the engineering team, or how well it is marketed, priced, and branded, the product will fail. If the functional requirements are on target, the rest will be a matter of execution, and the product has a fighting chance.

Product Marketing

The product marketer is the person who is responsible for gathering the data needed to answer these questions: What is out there? What problems are out there? Who out there is wrestling with these problems? What opportunities are out there to deliver value? Who would benefit from such value? How much are these users willing to pay for having their problems solved or from enjoying the value that a product could deliver? How many of such users are out there and how easy is it to find them? The product marketer needs to provide this information to the product manager so that the product manager can build a product that will solve real problems or deliver real value—a product that a large number of users are willing to pay for at a price that creates profit for the company or grows the company's market share in cases where growth is the company's main strategic consideration with that product.

The product marketer is also the team member who needs to collect information about the competition. What products and solutions are out there that people are using to solve their problem or enjoy value? It's important for the product marketer not to confine themselves to simply an analysis of "the competition." The competition—companies that are working on solving similar problems or delivering similar value—is only part of the competitive landscape. What the product marketer is after is answering the question, What products out there will be competing against my product once I release it? Products and solutions that exist and are not created by "the competition" that users are using to solve their problems are also part of a competitive analysis. For example, if you are building project-planning software, all-purpose spreadsheet software should be part of your product's competitive analysis, since the lowly spreadsheet is probably going to be your stiffest competition (people are comfortable using spreadsheets, they have invested a lot of time becoming experts in using them, etc.). It may also be your greatest opportunity, since the number of people using spreadsheets to keep track of their projects is much larger than the size of any of your competitor's customer base.

UX Research

Having identified the product's target end user, the product manager now needs to engage the UX researcher, whose job it is to gather data about such target end users out there. The product manager will—and can't help but—start with a general conception of who the target user is. The user may be the person in the household in charge of preparing meals, the senior who spends most of their days alone in the home, the college student who is trying to memorize some facts and figures, or toddlers who are learning how to feed themselves. It doesn't matter: whatever conception the product manager comes to the table with about the user, that conception is nothing but a starting point to a lot of work ahead that needs to be carefully done to bring the clarity and depth needed to deliver an actual product.

Three key questions that the UX researcher will help the product manager solve are:

What are the target users exactly trying to do?
> In other words, what is their real goal? This is the most crucial question to ask and answer. Not asking it, or answering it the wrong way, can lead the team to focus on constraining the solution opportunities.

What are the specific attributes that need to be identified to define the target users?
> These will prevent the designers from making incorrect assumptions when designing.

What is the context of their actions?
> Do the users have privacy when they are trying to solve the problem? Are they hard of hearing? Are they technologically savvy?

UX Design

This is the team that designs exactly what the voicebot says and how it acts. The UX designer, as we mentioned, needs to be very close to the product manager since the product manager is the one who will supply them with the list of functional requirements—*what* the user will need to be able to do when using the product. But equally important, the UX designer will need to stay close to the UX researcher, since the findings of the UX researcher will enable the designer to keep in mind the real-life constraints that the user must contend with when they use the product.

Development

Members of the development team, often referred to as "engineers," interact very closely with the product manager and the UX designer to understand what they are building and why they are building it.

The effective product manager understands that engineers are at their best when they are given the full context of the software they are building. If they know not only who the users are and what problems they will be solving but also have a sense of the product roadmap, how the product is likely to evolve, and where the product fits in the company's strategy, they will be able to make sound decisions about what development tools to use, what platforms to adopt, and what practices to follow; this ensures that they don't create technical debt (for instance, they didn't know that the product was a stepping-stone in a strategy that would take the user base size to the next order of magnitude, and hence scalability of the product should be an overriding concern from the beginning).

The engineer will also heavily interact with the UX designer, who is the owner of the detailed specifications the engineer will need to implement. It is the engineer's responsibility to:

- Go over the requirements in detail to ensure that they have the clarity they need to build according to those requirements.

- Call out any disconnects they may detect between what they heard or read from the product manager and what they are hearing or reading from the UX designer.

- Communicate to the product manager and the UX designer limitations and constraints that may get in the way of delivering according to the requirements; for instance, if engineering is constrained to using a service that is slow (e.g., looking up the details of a business establishment) and the UX design requires that the user obtain their answer within a shorter span of time than the service they are using can accommodate, the engineer is the one who needs to flag this disconnect and engage with the product manager and the UX designer about what to do. For example, the product manager can promise to secure a budget so the engineer can upgrade to faster service; or the UX designer needs to adjust their requirements and change their UX accordingly, to still deliver a highly usable experience within the technical and financial constraints.

Quality Engineering

Any team that aims to deliver a high-quality product needs to include a professionally trained team of quality engineers (QEs). The job of a QE is to ensure that the software developed by the engineering team meets the spirit as well as the details of the UX design. To be able to determine whether a piece of software meets the spirit of the design, the QE needs to be well-informed at the product level about what the product is supposed to do, who is using that product, and why they are using it. This information they should seek from the product manager. To ensure that the software meets the letter of the design document, the QE needs to be deeply familiar with the specific UX design requirements. It is based on this document that the QE will create their detailed test scripts. The QE owns responsibility to ensure that the UX requirements are as detailed as possible to enable the QE to create their test scripts. If they detect gaps, they should call them out.

A common, but major, mistake that teams make is to engage the QE team only once development has been completed and is now ready to be tested. The experienced QE team will insist on being involved as early in the process as possible. No development should begin before the QE team has reviewed functional requirements and the detailed UX requirements, deciding that those requirements are clear and detailed enough for the QE team to build test scripts. In fact, ideally, the QE team should begin building the test scripts before development begins and should have the tests ready before development ends.

To carry out their task effectively, the QE team should not be part of the software development team and should not answer or report to anyone within that team. They should also not be under the product team or the design team or report to anyone within those teams. The QE should be able to report issues, challenge requirements, and be as aggressive as they need to be to do their job. They should also be aware that their relationship with the software engineers will be complicated. No one likes having their mistakes pointed out, let alone logged and documented. Similarly, no one likes being shown that they were not clear in their communications or that their specifications were not detailed enough.

The effective QE is the one who is seen by the software engineer as that member of the team who is there to help them find bugs and issues *before* the software is delivered to the end user, and the one who ensures that the engineer has built according to the UX designer's requirements. The effective QE is the one who is seen by the UX designer as the one who is there to ensure that the engineer will build something that is exactly what the UX designer wanted built.

In terms of specific tasks, following are the four main types of testing that the QE engages in.

Functional Testing

The goal here is to ensure that the voicebot does what it is supposed to do. For instance, when the customer asks for the status of a shipment, the voicebot is providing accurate information and in such a way that it is delivered according to the UX requirements.

Traversal Testing

The goal here is to test every possible path that can be taken during a conversation between a human user and the voicebot.

For complex applications, automated testing may be the only way to execute a full traversal testing.

Stress Testing

This tests the platform's capacity to process spikes in engagement and voicebot system usage.

Beta Testing

Beta testing is the phase of the delivery process that takes place just before the product is generally launched into the real world.

This is where the product is placed in the hands of actual users—not members of the deployment team, or any team within the company, but actual end users.

To ensure that proper beta testing is conducted, it is essential to make sure that the beta testing manager does not report to any of the other members of the team or to any of the organizations within which those members work. The beta testing manager needs to have an agenda that answers to no other agenda. Their task is to identify where the product is falling short when placed in the hands of real users who have no vested interest in the success of the product.

The aim of the beta testing phase is to catch any issues that a real user may encounter—issues that may simply not be detected by anyone on the team simply because the team knows too much, is operating with unrecognized assumptions, or is more technically savvy than the real user.

The beta testing manager will work very closely with the product manager to ensure that the beta testers who will be enrolled in the testing are representative of the target user base that will use the product when the product is launched.

Program Management

If we were to liken a group of professionals working on the delivery of a product to a startup, we would liken a product manager to the founder/CEO: they are in charge of creating a vision, establishing a team, motivating that team, financing that team, and ensuring that a viable product is delivered to the market.

A crucial partner to the product manager is the program manager. If we were to liken them to an executive in a startup, they would be the chief operating officer (COO), the one who is in charge of making sure that plans are executed on time; roadblocks are anticipated and avoided, or at least identified and removed; and disputes between team members are resolved. To do their job well, the effective program manager must have a deep understanding of the vision that the product manager wishes to turn into a product. They need to have a clear view of the forest and they need to constantly keep that view clear. This is harder than it seems, given that the program manager's day-to-day job is to deal with trees, shrubbery, and whatever fauna they may encounter in their journey. But having a clear view of that forest will help the program manager make sure that everyone on the team is working with the right priorities in mind. Disputes, when they arise between team members (and they will always arise) need to be resolved by referring back to the question: What are we trying to do and why? There are times when the program manager, the skilled diplomat that they must be, will need to broker compromises; but such compromises should never be made at the expense of the vision. No feature should be added just to appease a member of the product team and no feature should be dropped just to appease a member of the engineering team. Is the UX research report that the UX researcher worked hard to put together being ignored by the product manager, who may be enamored with the vision they have and sure of themselves, and so does not bother to read UX findings? If so, it is the program manager's job to call out this failure and ensure that the UX report is read and signed off on by both the product manager and the UX designer, both of whom must take the UX research report seriously at the risk of building a product that no one will really need or want to use.

Here are some (but not all of) the other things that a program manager does: field complaints from members of the team about things like documentation shortcomings (vision statements, UX research reports, UX designs documents); manage blockages (a deliverable that is late and that a member of the team needs delivered before they can meet their own deadlines); deal with other members (disrespectful, incompetent, lazy); make sure that deadlines and timetables are reasonable; ensure that the team leads are getting along with one another; ensure that team members are not suffering from burnout; collect any information that will keep the delivery of the product on schedule and on spec in a way that is sustainable.

Like a good COO, the program manager needs to be sure that their CEO is always in the loop and that they are never blindsided by something they should have seen coming. And like a good COO, they need to make sure that the CEO does their job of empowering the team to be successful.

CHAPTER 24

Post-Launch Monitoring

No matter how deep your UX research has been, or how carefully your VUI was designed, how diligently the design was implemented, or how thoroughly the implementation was tested and beta certified, if your aim is to maintain a world-class, highly usable voice user experience, your voicebot will need regular and careful tuning once deployed to the real world. Robust and enduring excellence happens when a launched product is continuously evolving as information is collected about its use by real users.

Unfortunately, in the world of voicebots, *such post-launch tuning is almost never done in any serious way.*

Voicebots are launched and then life moves on. At best—but very rarely—quarterly analyses are conducted, and in those instances where they are conducted, concrete actions are almost never taken to improve the voicebot's usability, or add features to the voicebot, or even tweak it here and there to make it more effective. We, the authors, have witnessed project after project where the voicebot is not touched, not even once, for years and years, if ever.

Why is that the case? We believe the answer is simple: unlike a mobile app that crashes or an ugly website that has missing images and broken links that, say, an executive will bump into (and get infuriated about and then will order their marketing team to fix the problems posthaste), almost no one in the company—let alone executives—will ever bother to engage with the voicebot, and they certainly won't engage with it on a regular basis the way real users engage with a voicebot.

So, problem number one to solve if one is serious about delivering voicebot excellence is to make someone own the voicebot the way someone owns social media or owns the website. They need to be given metrics to report on, an opportunity to report on their findings with the same frequency as the one given to those who report on the website or social media; and their recommendations need to be acted upon with the same urgency and seriousness as those of other digital properties. Everyone must understand that real customers and real prospects are using the voicebot, and that during such interactions, the likelihood is high that the brand is taking a bad hit when the voicebot is not doing its job.

Sources of Information

To effectively tune your voicebot, you need to have at your disposal the following sources of information.

Interaction Logs

These are blow-by-blow accounts of what human users did and what the voicebot did. For instance, you should be able to tell from your logs what a user asked, what the voicebot said in response, whether such a response was correct or useful, or whether it was a no-input (the voicebot said that it didn't hear the user) or a no-match (the voicebot wasn't able to map what it heard to an intent).

The Audio of the Interactions

These are audio recordings of the users interacting with voice-bots. Such recordings provide rich information about the emotional state of the human (e.g., frustration, satisfaction), their cognitive state (e.g., confusion, surprise), as well as a better sense of how the voicebot sounds in real life with real people. For instance, it may turn out that the voicebot is speaking certain important words or phrases in a way that is not easy to understand by users, or they are speaking for too long, or they are coming across as cheerful as they deliver bad news. The more audio you can obtain, whether about end-to-end interactions or snippets of audio, the richer your understanding will be of how the voicebot is doing and where trouble spots may be found.

End Users

The best thing you can do for your voicebot once it is launched is to view the post-launch period as nothing more than an indefinite period of beta testing. The voicebot is out, but it is never done. It is always a work in progress.

As we mentioned, rare is the team that does this, but rare also is excellence, and rarer still is delight. If you want to have a voicebot like no other, then examine it with the same intensity as you did when it was going through a beta test phase. Regularly engage with real users. Ask them the questions you asked the beta testers. Unearth new questions. Identify new opportunities and keep a prioritized list of issues, enhancements, and new features to implement.

The Basic Questions

Following are the basic questions that need to be asked in order to begin tuning a voice application.

Where Are Users Abandoning the Session?

An explicit termination (the user said "Stop" or "Quit") or an implicit one (the user stops responding) prior to completing a task (say, receiving the status of an order) are usually signs of user frustration or dissatisfaction with the voicebot.

Where Are Users Asking to Be Connected to a Human Agent?

If you have designed your voicebot with the goal of empowering the user to serve themselves, you must provide the user with the option to be connected to a human agent. A user actively asking to speak to an agent is a user who has decided (fairly or not) that the voicebot is not successfully enabling them to serve themselves. This is especially true of users who have engaged the voicebot over several minutes of interaction and then decided to bail out.

Where Are Users Saying the Wrong Things?

The aim here is to identify those spots in your voicebot's interactions where no-match failures are significantly higher than the average rate in the rest of the interaction. Where audio recordings are available, one useful practice is to listen to the prompt the user hears and then listen to what users are saying in response to that prompt. In such situations, adjust your voicebot by either rewriting the prompt or strengthening the language the voicebot is expecting the user to say.

Where Are Users Not Saying Anything?

These are the spots in your voicebot interactions where users do not respond at all to a voicebot request. This can happen for several reasons:

- The voicebot's prompt is confusing.
- The user was asked for information they don't have and can't easily provide or can't provide at all (for instance,

they are asked for their passport number, but their passport is in a box in their bank, or they don't have a passport).

- The user has the information, but they just need a bit of time to fetch it (for instance, their driver's license number).

- The user has the information with them, but they are slow in providing it (they speak hesitantly and slowly or they can't easily read the small print).

If the issue is with lack of clarity of ambiguity, then recraft your prompt. If the issue is with lack of readiness, and this lack of readiness is prevalent among users of your voicebot, then one effective strategy is to let the user know from the start of the interaction what pieces of information they will be asked to provide during the exchange and to offer them the option to terminate the action and come back later when they are ready. Be sure to announce this early in the interaction so that you avoid wasting the user's time (and frustrating them). You don't want them interacting with the voicebot for several minutes, only to be told they need some document they may not have with them and be forced to start the interaction all over again.

If the user was told at the outset of the exchange what they need and yet still are not able to provide the information because they need some time to retrieve it, add to your VUI the ability to pause the conversation (e.g., by playing music, for instance, while they are retrieving the needed information).

Where Are Users Speaking Too Soon?

At times, users are impatient and speak sooner than they should, often missing crucial information or instructions. This is usually an indication that the prompt was not designed optimally. For instance, if your prompt starts with a question the user can answer and then provides qualification to that question, reword the prompt by putting the question last. For instance, instead of having your voicebot saying: "What's your dorm room number? Please make sure you start by giving me the dorm name," a prompt that is less likely to result in the user speaking too soon is, "I need two things from you: your dorm name followed by your dorm room number."

What Is the Noise Level of Your User's Environment?

When you listen to audio recordings of interactions between humans and voicebots, pay attention to the noise level and how such noise is affecting the no-match error rates. If your voicebot can tell that a person is engaging them from a noisy environment, then ask them to go to a quieter place during a no-match event. If you discover that most people are engaging the voicebot from a noisy environment, then make your ask at the opening prompt and occasionally when a no-match event is triggered. You may also want to go back to the drawing board and ask yourself and your team: is a voicebot the best interface for users in this case, if most of them are engaging it in a noisy environment? It may turn out that the answer is still yes, but it may turn out that, no, a voicebot is not the best way.

What Options Are Your Users Asking For?

If you discover that 80% of your users are engaging the voicebot primarily to check their savings balance, then from the very outset of the interaction, ask 100% of the users if they wish to be given their savings balance. By definition, 80% of the time you will be right.

How Are Users Feeling About the Voicebot?

You can probably get a good sense of how users feel about your voicebot by just listening to the tone of their voice in the audio recordings. Most will patiently endure, but even they convey in the tone of their spoken responses how they feel. A few will be vocal in their dissatisfaction and will curse at your voicebot or make side comments. Note down two things: *where* exactly in the conversation such dissatisfaction was expressed and *how* exactly such dissatisfaction was expressed. The former will help you begin to figure out why the user was dissatisfied (maybe it was a confusion prompt) and the latter how intense was the emotion (a grunt versus profanity). Also note places where the user expresses satisfaction and how that satisfaction was expressed (i.e., the user says a cheerful, "Wow! Thank you!").

CHAPTER 25

The Elements of Voice First Success

Like any other tool, a voicebot is successful only to the extent that it solves a user's problem or delivers a utility that the user seeks to extract from it.

However, knowing exactly whether or not a user's problem has been solved or if the user was able to enjoy the value they sought in the voicebot is often difficult. Instead, it is far easier to assess how a voicebot is performing in the aggregate by tracking a few key behaviors and outcomes.

The following sections are a list of metrics that collectively measure the effectiveness of a voicebot. Note that the exact meaning of many of these metrics is seldom obvious. Such meaning often needs to be negotiated with multiple stakeholders. For instance, when should we say that a user has "abandoned" a voicebot session? When should we say they have "completed a task"? And what is a "task" in the first place? Unless these terms are defined clearly, identifying points of success and failure will be difficult, and the conversations about what to do to improve the voicebot (its usability, its effectiveness, etc.) will be frustratingly elusive.

Abandonment Rate

The abandonment rate refers to the proportion of sessions where users abandoned the voicebot before completing *any* task. For instance, if a voicebot offers the user the ability to hear information about restaurant hours, nearest location, and the special on the menu that day, and the user does not pick any of the options and simply terminates their interaction with the voicebot, then we can say that the user abandoned the session. If the user were to ask for the nearest location but then did not answer the voicebot's question, "What is your zip code?" and instead said "Stop" or "Goodbye," then we can say that the user abandoned the session.

Automation Rate

The automation rate is the proportion of sessions where users were able to complete at least one task within the voicebot. Among other targets, the metric can apply to a specific task, set of tasks, user population, or set of sessions. For instance, one may look at the automation rate across all users for the store locator task. One may look at the rate of automation of all the tasks taken together for all users. Or one may decide to assess the rate of automation of users who engage with the voicebot on a weekday compared to those who engage with it during the weekend, or only for one specific task across all users. It's up to the business leaders to decide what automation rates to measure that best help them draw meaningful conclusions and take rational action where needed.

Average Number of Failures per Session

This metric is an effective way to assess how well a voicebot is doing with its users. Obviously, the larger the average number of failures per session (no-input and no-match errors), the less satisfied users will be.

Average Number of Failures per Task

This metric is a measure of the effectiveness of the voicebot for enabling the completion of a specific task. Again, obviously, the larger the average number of errors a user encounters as they try to solve a task, the less satisfied the users will be.

Average Task Completion Time

The average task completion time is the average time taken by users to complete a given task. In the context of transactional voicebots—where the goal is to help users complete tasks as quickly as possible—the longer time a user takes to complete a task, the less likely they are to be satisfied with the voicebot. That is why, length of completion tasks positively correlate with abandonment rates. Reduce the time it takes users to complete tasks and you are likely to see the abandonment rate drop.

Containment Rate

In situations where the voicebot can connect the user with a human agent, the containment rate is that subset of sessions between the human and the voicebot that did not result in a transfer of the user to a human agent.

Note that containment rate by itself is not a reliable indicator of the usability of the implemented voicebot. A user may be "contained," but they may have abandoned the session. Or they may have completed their task but took a long time to complete that task. In other words, always seek to increase the containment without increasing the abandonment rate or decreasing the task completion rate.

First-Use Resolution Rate

First-use resolution rate refers to the proportion of conversations between the user and the voicebot where the user was able to accomplish their goal and where the user had not

---

previously engaged with the voicebot unsuccessfully in their attempt to accomplish that goal. ("First-time-final" and "once-and-done" are also terms that are used for this metric.)

Task Completion Rate

The task completion rate refers to the proportion of sessions where the user completed a given task they engaged the voice-bot to accomplish.

Task Initiation Rate

The task initiation rate is the proportion of sessions where users initiated a task in the voicebot. This is more of a measure of customer engagement with the voicebot (compared to, for instance, a user who listens to the opening prompt and a list of menu options and then abandons the session) and by itself is not a reliable indicator of task completion. Knowing that the initiation rate of a task is high, but that its completion is low, is usually an indication that the user interface was not well designed.

Time to Task

Time to task is the time elapsed between the beginning of a session and the time when the user is given the conversational turn (the time they get to say something) and are able to initiate a task. As mentioned many times before, a best practice is to get the user engaged as soon as possible. Hence, all things being equal, comparing two voicebots, the one with the lower time to task is better than the one with the higher one.

CHAPTER 26

Coda

Building voicebots is a craft, and if you want to learn a craft you must practice it every single day. No book or manual, no matter how good, can ever replace actual practice. You must create from scratch and learn from both your mistakes and your successes. But mainly from your mistakes. A manual can at best provide you with concepts and describe tricks and techniques. It can help you figure out where to start and how to start, how to formulate a strategy for tackling problems and, when it is a really good manual, it can help you ask the right questions. But by itself, a manual is never enough. You will not be able to build a great voicebot by simply reading this book, or any book.

Building great voicebots—as is the case with building anything that will survive the real world—is hard. It requires years of patient learning by doing. If you want to become a great voicebot professional, make sure that *you are always in the process of building a voicebot*. This means thinking about things like: How do I structure a sequence? How do I craft a prompt? How do I ensure that the user knows how to get the conversation back on track when it goes sideways? How do I get the voicebot to understand what the user is trying to do? and How do I make it as easy as possible for the user to do what they want to do with the voicebot? But you must do much more than simply think. You must also *try things out*: i.e., *talk* to your voicebot, *listen* to how it responds, how it sounds, what it says, how long it takes to say what it says, and then, crucially, talk to users and members of your team. If your actual, paying job is to build voicebots, then you are in a great spot: you are practicing your craft and learning every day while making a living from it. It can't get better than that. But if you are not a professional voicebot builder—yet—and you don't get a chance to build every day, and you want to become a professional voicebot builder, then find a way to be building *every single day*. Yes, easier said than done, but just as a writer—if they want to call themselves a real writer—must write every single day and must do so whether or not they are being paid to write, or what sort of a day they are having on any given day, the same with you. *Be in the process of building a voicebot every single day*. If you are not doing it, then perhaps you are not serious about becoming a professional voicebot builder.

But what does it mean to *always be in the process of building a voicebot*? How does one go about doing this, in concrete, practical terms?

Here's our suggestion. Find two more people who want to get into the voice first business and partner with them to build great voicebots. Commit one year of your life to building four voicebots, each voicebot taking three months to build and launch *into the real world*. Not in a lab, or to friends, but into the real world. Follow this process and after that one year, if you work very hard, you will grow as a voicebot professional and you will be taken seriously by those who are looking for voicebot professionals.

Why would you be taken seriously? First, you will be able to show a portfolio of artifacts. Depending on what role you assumed in the projects, they could be UX research reports, functional requirement documents, code, test scripts, beta program plans and reports, and post-launch analysis reports. Combine this with your understanding of the process, the fact that you actually invested one whole year of your life in learning by doing, that you worked with a team, and that you delivered—this combination will turn you into a formidable candidate: "This is someone who has their act together; they can set up goals, work hard, work well with others, think strategically, are ambitious, and deliver concrete results." A hiring manager cannot ask for more. And the key thing is this: these are not your mere assertions, or the mere assertions of your references. These are assertions that the hiring manager is making by looking at your output, the reality of which cannot be doubted or denied.

Specifically, here's one methodology that we have found works well—one that we have coined as *The One Pizza Methodology*—for establishing a team and dividing the labor among the members of that team to deliver on your one year of work to build your portfolio.

But before we describe this methodology, some quick history first. In the early days, Amazon's Jeff Bezos instituted a rule whereby every internal team was to be small enough that it could be fed with two pizzas. The philosophy: a smaller team spends less time handling schedules and managing people and more time getting done what needs to be done.

The One Pizza Methodology we are proposing here is a variation of Amazon's two-pizza rule, and it consists in bringing together groups of three people, all passionately interested in professionally entering the voice first world. Why three people? Because that's the number of people that a large pizza (with toppings that none of the three members objects to) can feed.

The three members of the one-pizza team occupy the following roles, one member per role:

- Product manager
- UX designer
- Software developer

The team's task is to:

- Identify a *specific problem* or a *specific opportunity* that a well-defined target user, or someone else interested in solving the target user's problem, is willing to pay money for with a voice first solution to that problem or for the fulfillment of that opportunity.
- Design a voice first app that solves the problem or delivers on the opportunity.
- Build that voice app.
- Test it.
- Beta test it.
- Market it and launch it.
- Monitor it after launch.

Here is what the individual members of the team would do:

- UX research: product manager
- Functional requirements definition: product manager
- UX-detailed design: UX designer
- Development: software developer
- Testing: product manager and UX designer
- Beta testing: product manager and UX designer
- Marketing communications & branding: product manager
- Monitoring: product manager

Following are the artifacts the team should produce. Make sure that you don't skimp on these artifacts. Aside from your ability to explain and articulate what you did, they will be the only concrete evidence of your work:

- UX research report
- Functional requirements document

- UX-detailed design document
- Code base
- Testing scripts
- Test reports
- Published reviews of the voice app
- Marketing plan
- Launch plan
- Awards that the voice app may have won
- The actual app itself, published and available for real use

With your passion, with this book in hand, your voice first team by your side, an immovable tenacity, and one year of hard work, you *will* become a voicebot professional.

Work hard. Have fun. And make great voicebots.

The 10 Sources of Voice First Failures!

The doom of a voicebot project can often be predicted before any work is done; just examine the team that is tasked to deliver the voicebot and the processes this team will be using. Here are 10 such indicators that should set off your alarms if you find yourself working on deploying a voicebot:

- *Not treating the voicebot as a product* and not assigning a product manager to lead it from beginning to end. A voicebot that has no owner who will be celebrated if it succeeds or blamed if it fails is a voicebot that *will* fail.

- *Designing from the armchair*, without discovery, without identifying the actual target user, without identifying the business buyer, without gathering the key people involved in establishing the business purpose and fleshing out the requirements.

- *Treating the voicebot deployment as if it were an IT project* and handing ownership of it to the engineering team.

- *Grossly under financing the voicebot project*, while spending an order of magnitude or two more on the mobile app, the website, social media, and videos.

- *Not hiring VUI professionals*. Yes, we are all experts in carrying conversations. But that does not mean we can design voice first experiences between a human being and a voicebot. We don't pretend to be writers just because we can write, or that we can hop into a race car just because we have been driving cars for decades. Why do we think we can design a voicebot just because we can converse? A corollary of this failure: *Micromanaging* the VUI designer and second-guessing them. When nondesigners start insisting on certain wordings, then they are asking for usability trouble.

- *Using internal employees to record prompts*. A nonprofessional voice actor is much worse than text-to-speech software because they will come across as *people who are speaking unnaturally*. If the voicebot comes across as not sounding completely natural, that is understandable. But why did the brand not bother to record the prompts using professional talent? Is it because the brand can't afford it? Are they financially strapped? Or is it that they don't care about the customer experience? Or is it because they don't care about their brand? Whatever the reason, amateur recording does not reflect well on the brand.

- *Letting Legal or Marketing have their way* instead of figuring out how to satisfy their needs without compromising the voice user experience. For instance, speaking long disclaimers at the opening prompt rather than delivering such a disclaimer in some other way (via text or email).

- *Not training customer care agents and managers on the voicebot* and what it can or can't do before it is deployed.

- Altogether *skipping the beta testing phase*.

- *Not monitoring the performance of the voicebot* after deployment and not refining and adapting the voicebot to new findings.

Demonstrating Voice First

If you have ever given demos of voicebots, you know how stressful the experience can be. You have put on your best Sunday suit and done all the right things: behaved impeccably, given a great PowerPoint presentation, demonstrated full and sensitive understanding of your prospect's problems, definitely impressed your prospect with your client list and the reference quotes, and more. But all that, you fear—as you get ready to give your voicebot demo—could be wiped out (or so it feels when it happens) with a cruel, "I'm sorry, I didn't understand that!"

When you are demoing, remember that your goal is *not* to show off technology but rather to show off *your company's all-around competence*: your competence as a businessperson and as someone who knows the product they are selling, and the competence of the team that put together the product—in this case, the voicebot.

Needless to say, your demo is as good as the VUI design behind it—and a solid design is your starting point. The key thing is this: the voicebot being demoed was designed for a use case that is *not* the same as the use case of the one who is demoing it—that is, the user for whom the voicebot was built is *not* looking to demo the competence of the company that built and sold it, but to solve their problem. This is an important point to keep in mind simply because a highly usable voicebot for an end user may not demo very well.

Remove All Prompts That Explicitly Talk About Failure

When demoing a voicebot, remove prompts such as: "I'm sorry, I didn't understand that" or, "Sorry, I didn't hear you." Instead, you could use a double beep, which will cue you to speak again (and could be interpreted by your audience as a failure on your end rather than the technology's), or just reprompt.

Don't Speak Over Prompts

Instead, wait for the prompt to complete, or at least wait for a pause and then speak your answer. Obviously, make sure that when your demo's VUI has such pauses and silences, they are long enough to let you speak your answer or interrupt.

Don't Have the Voicebot Talk for More Than 10 Seconds When It Starts Without Giving the Turn Back to You

Nothing spoils the mood of a demo like a lengthy, tedious prompt. For some reason, time passes by very slowly during a voice first demo. Keep that in mind.

Test the Voicebot with the Same Equipment You Will Use in the Demo

If you are demoing your voicebot on a smart speaker, test it on a smart speaker—and the exact smart speaker you will be demoing on. If it's a Google Mini you will be using, test it on a

Google Mini. If it's an Amazon Echo Show, test it on the Echo Show. If it's a regular landline or a cell phone, do likewise.

Have Two or Three Backup Ways to Demo the Voicebot

Never go into a situation without at least one backup plan for what to do if your primary plan fails. And the more backup plans, the better. Bring a Google Mini, an Amazon Echo Show, an Amazon Echo Dot, your smartphone, and, if all else fails— say, the WiFi is dead—have a video or an audio recording of the demo on your laptop or smartphone. None of the preparation, when things go wrong, will go unnoticed by your audience. Someone who comes this prepared to a meeting works at a company where the people are professional and serious. Again, you are selling not just the voicebot but the competence of the company as a whole.

Test the Application in the Same Room and Environment Where You Will Do the Demo

Ambient acoustics can make a big difference, even if your ears can't tell. Show up to the meeting where you are demoing early. If the demo is virtual, make sure you test it ahead of time in the same room, with the same WiFi configuration, where you will be demoing it.

Know How to Gracefully End a Telephony- Based Voicebot

If the voicebot you are demoing is a telephony-based one and you are conferencing in the voicebot, make sure you know how to end the voicebot without needing to kill the whole conference call.

Ask for Silence

Make sure to tell everyone in the room, and the room or conference line, to remain quiet or to mute while you demo.

Never Improvise or Show Off While Demoing

The purpose of your demo is not to show off but to provide the outlines of a vision of what the customer will be getting. So, make sure you pick a path in the conversation flow, ensure that the path works every time you traverse it by testing it several times, and then, during the demo, traverse it exactly as you had tested it.

If, for Whatever Reason, the Voicebot Fails, Be Honest About Why It Failed

There are many reasons why a voicebot fails even though you have prepared assiduously: it could be because the WiFi is bad, or the backend to which the voicebot is connected failed, or you deviated from the demo path and so were touching points in the voicebot flow that you hadn't tested. Whatever the reason, the best policy is to quickly come clean and then to play the recorded demo. The audience will appreciate your honesty, they will be impressed that you had a backup plan, and they will appreciate your leadership in getting the group out of an uncomfortable situation: you kept your cool, understood what was happening, explained it, and then moved on with your plan B.

No Cheat Sheets!

Know how to use your voicebot without having to rely on any printouts or other visual aids (like having the script on your smartphone). You can have such visuals to help you pre-pare, but don't demo while looking at a cheat sheet or your smartphone. This will make you look lazy, and the voicebot will come across as complex—since it needs instructions to use!

Speak Normally

Often, when a voicebot doesn't understand something, users repeat what they said by speaking unnaturally: either slowly or loudly or both. This usually doesn't help (in fact, it makes things worse). Instead, you should speak in a normal voice and at a natural volume. Not only will this be more likely to result in the voicebot understanding you but will make you look cool and composed.

Don't Leave Long Silences Between Words When You Speak

As technology stands today, voicebots can't tolerate more than 1.5 seconds of silence between spoken words in the incoming speech they are listening to and will interpret the gap as an end-of-speech event (you have stopped talking). So, know your demo and avoid long pauses.

Keep It Really Short

Make sure you don't have the voicebot speak for more than 10 seconds (at the very most) without giving the turn back to you. People (especially people visiting an expo booth, for instance) are impatient with voice demos. A short duration (3–5 seconds) of the assistant speaking is ideal. You are going after quick interactions, creating an impression, painting a vision, and making a point, so that you can move along to the conversation between you and the prospect.

Useful Matrices

The Assessment Matrix Cheat Sheet

Use this cheat sheet to quickly assess the quality of a voicebot.

Functionality
What does the voicebot do and does it deliver concrete value to the user? If you can explain this value in one short sentence, then you have started with a good foundation. Here's an example of well-defined functionality: "This voicebot helps you remove stains on your shirt." Another one: "This voicebot gives you tips on how to cook a great spaghetti meal." Here's an example of a not-so-good functionality statement: "This voicebot helps you use Tide products." Here's another one: "This voicebot is your meal preparation companion."

Modality fit
Is the target use case a good fit for voice and voicebots? Start with the basic question: given the use case, can the user do this just as easily, or even more easily using, say, a smartphone? If the answer is yes, then the modality fit is probably weak.

Invocation
In the case of far-field speech, how easy is it for someone to start an interaction with the voicebot? Do they need to remember a name—e.g., a wake word followed by the name of the voicebot? If so, how easy is that wake word/voicebot name combination to remember? Can it be made easier?

Closing	When you say "Quit," "Stop," or "Goodbye," does the voicebot stop or does it go on talking? For example: "Great. I hope I was able to help you. Thank you for using Coffee Mugs Are Us. Please visit us at www.coffeemugsareus.com. That's www.coffeemugsareus.com. Bye!"
Brevity	How long are the prompts?
Help	Does it offer actionable help?
Questions	Does it ask questions clearly and in a way that enables the customer to know what to say?
Cognitive load	How many things does the voicebot require the user to remember at any time during the conversation?
Failure recovery strategies	How well does the voicebot handle no-input (the user doesn't say anything) and no-match (the user says something out of scope) failures?
Speech recognition accuracy	How often does the voicebot not recognize something that it should recognize?
Perceived latency	How fast does the voicebot respond? And if it doesn't respond quickly, does it use mitigating strategies, such as "Please wait while I retrieve the information for you" and/or play background sound that makes it clear that the voicebot is in the process of formulating a response?
Text-to-Speech (TTS)	Does the voicebot pronounce things incorrectly? For instance, how well does it handle heterophones such as "close," "object," or "present"?
Information architecture	Do the steps follow an order that makes sense to the user? Was there care put in in the presentation of the information?

Value-Usability Matrix

If you are a VUI designer or a product manager, this is a handy matrix you should hang on your wall. Try to always build for the "Love!" quadrant. This is represented by the top right square in Figure C-1. Build voicebots that are exquisitely crafted and deliver value to users. All other squares should be no-go zones.

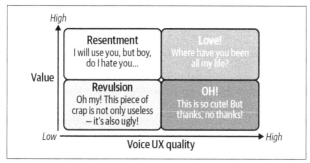

Figure C-1. Value-usability matrix

Feature Expectation Matrix

This matrix (Figure C-2) should be especially useful to the UX researcher and the product manager.

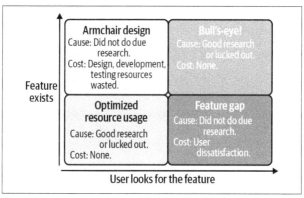

Figure C-2. Feature expectation matrix

Automation-Complexity Matrix

Whether to build and what to build for what situation is as crucial, if not more crucial, thank ensuring that what is built is usable. Build a voicebot when the task is complex and you get not only dissatisfied users, but also unhappy agents who have two engage with angry or irritated users who had to suffer through the bad voicebot. Build a voicebot that handles simple tasks, and you have happy users (they were able to quickly serve themselves rather than waste their time waiting) as well as happy agents (the get to deal only with solving problems that require their skills rather than problems that a voicebot could easily solve).

In this matrix, we describe the four possible Automation-Complexity scenarios (Figure C-3).

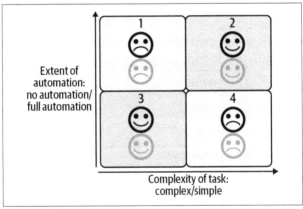

Figure C-3. Automation-complexity matrix

Quadrant 1

In this case, the user, who needs to engage in a complex task with a voicebot, is most likely going to be unhappy. In the world of telephony IVRs, such voicebots are often met with "transfer to agent" or zero-pressing. Human agents, for their part, are not happy because the voicebot is trying to do their job—and no one likes being displaced by a robot. They are also likely to be unhappy dealing with irritated users who are usually going to be asked to repeat information they had already provided to the voicebot.

Quadrant 2

The situation when everyone is happy. The user gets to serve themselves quickly and the agent is spared from doing mindless tasks.

Quadrant 3

This quadrant is also a happy place. This is the situation where the user has been connected with a competent human agent who enjoys helping solve complex problems a voicebot would be hard-pressed to solve.

Quadrant 4

For this one, the user is usually happy, unless they were made to wait, only to ask the human agent to do something that a simple voicebot could have done—for instance, activate their credit card. The human agent on the other end is also not so thrilled since they are being asked to do something that a simple voicebot can do.

A Voice First Glossary

acoustic model

A representation that maps the relationship between a digital signal to that of human spoken audio and the *phonemes* (*see term*) and other markers that describe various linguistic characteristics of that audio. Models are built based on sets of audio recordings and human transcription of such recordings.

activation phrase

What the user says to activate a voice first device, for instance, "Hey Google" to wake up a Google smart speaker or a smartphone.

adaptive system

A system that adapts its behavior to changing parameters, such as the user's identity, time of day, day of the week or month, context of the interaction, etc.

adjacency pair

A term used in linguistics to refer to two utterances by two speakers during a conversation, one after the other. For example, "Are you ready to start the survey?" followed by "Yes!" or "Would you like to subscribe to the service?" followed by "Nope!" are adjacency pairs.

affordance

A term that refers to an action potential that presents itself to a user of an object as a result of the object's shape or form or some other physical property that the user perceives as enabling them to do something with the object. A button invites a user to push it, while a stairway handle invites the user to hold it while climbing up or down the stairs.

always-listening device

A device that is always listening for a *wake word* and that sends the audio captured after the wake word has been detected for additional processing.

anaphora

The use of a grammatical substitute (such as a pronoun or a pro-verb) to refer to a word used earlier in a sentence, to avoid repetition. For instance, in the sentence "The shoes were a bit pricey, but I still bought them," the pronoun *them* is used to refer to *the shoes*.

ASR

Automatic speech recognition, or automatic speech recognizer. Usually this refers to software that is able to take audio input and map that input to a word or language utterance.

ASR tuning

The activity of iteratively configuring the ASR software to better map, both in accuracy and speed, the audio input to a word or an utterance.

barge-in

The ability of the user to interrupt system prompts while those prompts are being played. If barge-in is enabled in an application, then as soon as the user begins to speak, the system stops playing its prompt and begins processing the user's input.

cooperative principle

The proposition that listeners and speakers must act cooperatively and mutually accept one another to be understood in a particular way to carry out an effective verbal conversation. As phrased by British philosopher of language Paul Grice, who introduced it, "Make your contribution such as is required, at the stage at which it occurs, by the accepted purpose or direction of the talk exchange in which you are engaged."[1]

deixis

A term used in linguistics for the use of general words and phrases to refer to a specific time, place, or person in a given context. For instance, the words *next Saturday*, *here*, and *she* are deictic because their semantic meaning is fixed but their denoted meaning varies depending on time and/or place.

directed dialogue

Interactions where the exchange between the user and the system is guided by the application: the system asks questions or offers options and the user responds to them. Directed dialogues stand in contrast to "mixed initiative" dialogues, since they require the user to specifically answer the question asked and won't accept any other piece of information, whether additive (the user provided an answer to the question, but also an additional piece of information) or substitutive (the user provided instead an altogether different piece of information that is relevant and will be asked for by the system at some point).

disambiguation

The challenge of identifying what a user meant to say when they spoke a work or an utterance. For example, if a user gives only a city name during an exchange about

---

1 Paul Grice, "Logic and Conversation," in *Syntax and Semantics*, vol. 3, *Speech Acts*, ed. P. Cole and J. Morgan (Academic Press, 1975), 41–58.

booking a trip, was the city name the departure city or the destination city?

discovery

The process of learning what a system can do.

disfluency

Verbal utterances such as *ah*, *hmm*, etc., exhibited by speakers when hesitating or claiming retention of a speaking dialogue turn.

earcon

The audio equivalent of an icon in graphical user interfaces. Earcons are used to signal conversation marks (e.g., when the system starts listening, when the system stops listening) as well as to communicate brand, mood, and emotion during a voice first-based interaction.

Echo (Amazon Echo)

A far-field device released by Amazon in November 2014. *Echo* has also come to represent the Amazon-branded category of devices (Echo Dot, Echo Tap, Echo Look, Echo Show) that interact with Amazon Alexa cloud service.

echo cancellation

A technique that filters out audio coming out of a device while processing incoming audio for speech recognition into that same device. By being "aware" of the audio signal that it itself is generating, a system processing an audio signal that includes that signal along with, say, spoken audio from a user, would then be able to process more accurately the signal coming from the user.

end-pointing

The marking of the start and the end of a speaker's utterance for the purposes of ASR processing.

false accept

An instance where the ASR mistakenly accepted an utterance as a valid response.

false reject

An instance where the ASR mistakenly rejected an utterance as an invalid response.

far-field speech recognition

Speech recognition technology that is able to process speech spoken by a user from a distance (usually 10 feet away or more) to the receiving device, usually in a context where there is ambient noise. The first performing mainstream far-field speech recognition device and system was Amazon Echo. In contrast, technology that handles speech recognition on handheld, mobile devices (e.g., Siri) is called *near-field speech recognition* (*see term*).

Gricean maxims

A set of specific rational principles observed by people who obey the *cooperative principle* (*see term*). These principles enable effective verbal conversational communication between humans. British philosopher of language Paul Grice proposed four conversational maxims: quality, quantity, relevance, and manner.

Gutenberg Parenthesis

The proposition that the last 500 years or so—the time between the invention of typeset printing, which ushered in the era of the written word as the main mode of communicating knowledge, and the recent arrival of distributed social media—is a short parenthesis in a history of human communication that has relied on informal and decentralized communication. This communication was in oral form prior to Gutenberg (ca. 1400–1468) and currently via social media and orally.

heteronym

Two words are said to be heteronyms of each other if they share the same spelling but different pronunciations and meanings. For example, *tear* can refer to the salty liquid that comes out of one's eye when crying, or the act of ripping apart a piece of paper. Heteronyms are especially challenging for text-to-speech technology, where a word may be mispronounced by the software if the software's model heavily prefers one pronunciation over the other or is not provided enough context to enable it to determine the right pronunciation.

homonym

Two words are said to be homonyms of each other if they share the same spelling and the same pronunciation but mean different things. For instance, *cast* can mean a collection of people in a movie, but it can also mean something that is formed into a mold.

interaction design

The set of activities and strategies used to design digital products that involve a user interacting with an interface—for instance, someone playing a game on their smartphone or someone speaking to their smart speaker in a back-and-forth exchange. The key concern in interaction design is action that takes the user from one state to a new state. This is different from, say, designing a logo or an opening chime for a voicebot, where the design does not involve a state change.

mixed-initiative dialogue

Interactions where the user may unilaterally issue a request rather than simply provide exactly the information asked for by system prompts. For instance, while making a flight reservation, the system may ask the user, "What day are you planning to fly out?" Instead of answering that question, the user may say, "I'm flying to Denver, Colorado." A mixed-initiative system would recognize that the user provided not the exact answer to the question asked, but also (additive), or instead (substitutive), volunteered information that was going to be requested by the system later. Such a system would accept this information, remember it, and continue the conversation. In contrast, a *directed dialogue (see term)* system would rigidly insist on the departure date and wouldn't proceed successfully unless it received that piece of information.

multimodality

A user is said to be able to interact with a device multimodally if they are able to use more than one form of interaction: for instance, one can touch the surface of the iPhone but also look at images, listen to audio, and feel vibrations. Each one of these ways of consuming information is a modality. In the case of a voice-only user interface, the user is able to only speak and hear. Smart speakers are usually multimodal in that way (only audio), but many are augmented with visuals such as lights and screen.

N-Best

In speech recognition, given an audio input, an ASR returns a list of results, with each result ascribed a "confidence score" (usually a fraction between 0 and 1 (e.g., 0.87 or a percentage). N-Best refers to the N results that were returned by the ASR and were above the confidence threshold. For instance, if the user said, "Austin," and the recognizer were to return, "Austin" with a score of 0.92, "Boston" with 0.87, "Houston" with 0.65, "Aspen" with 0.52, and "Oslo" with 0.43, and the threshold were set at 0.55, the three best would be "Austin," "Boston," and "Houston." If the threshold were set at 0.70, only the first two, "Austin" and "Boston," would be returned. If the threshold were set to 0.40, the three best would still be "Austin," "Boston," and "Houston." The four best with a threshold of 0.40 would be "Austin," "Boston," "Houston," and "Aspen."

natural language processing (NLP)

Technology that extracts the meaning of a user's utterance or typed text. A meaning usually consists of an "intent" and "name-value" pair. The utterance "I want to book a flight from Washington, DC, to Boston" has the intent of "book a flight" with the name-value pairs being "Departure City" = "Washington, DC" and "Arrival City" = "Boston, MA." An NLP system takes the flat sequence of words, "I want to book a flight from Washington, DC, to Boston," and produces a *meaning structure* (usually a JSON object) that boils down the sequence of words to an intent and name-value pairs. The JSON object delivered can then be inspected by what is often called *middleware software* that can now easily extract the information in the object and execute additional business logic (e.g., retrieve available flight information; or ask for additional missing information, as in "What date would you be flying out of Washington, DC?").

near-field speech recognition
In contrast to far-field speech recognition, which processes speech spoken by a human to a device from a distance (usually 10 feet or more), near-field speech recognition technology is used for handing spoken input from handheld mobile devices (e.g., Siri on the iPhone) that are used within inches or up to two feet away at most.

no-input error
A situation where the system did not detect any speech input from the user.

no-match error
A situation where the system was not able to match the user's response to the responses that it expected the user to provide.

out-of-scope (OOS) error
See *no-match error.*

persona
The personality of the system (formal, playful, chatty, aggressive, friendly, etc.) that comes across when the system engages with the user. The persona is influenced by factors such as the perceived gender of the system, the type of language the system uses, and how the system handles errors.

phatic

A term used in linguistics to refer to a communication that serves primarily a social function rather than a semantic one. For instance, saying "Bless you!" after someone sneezes, or "You're welcome" in answer to "Thank you," are phatic communications.

phoneme

A term used in linguistics to refer to the smallest unit of speech distinguishing one word (or word element) from another. For instance, *b*, *p*, and *t* in the words *bad*, *bat*, and *pat*.

pragmatics

In linguistics, one of the three main branches of inquiry, the other two being *syntax* and *semantics* (*see terms*). Pragmatics is concerned with the social meaning of utterances. If a child tells their parent, "I'm hungry," the surface semantic meaning of the child's utterance is a declarative phrase that describes the hunger state of the child. But the real intention of the child speaking the utterance is to make a request, the request to be fed. This second meaning is the pragmatic meaning of the utterance.

progressive prompting

The technique of beginning an exchange by providing the user with minimal instructions and elaborating on those instructions only if encountering response errors (e.g., no-input, no-match, etc.).

prompt

The instruction or response that a system "speaks" to the user.

prosody

In linguistics, prosody is concerned with the properties of syllables, such as intonation, stress, and rhythm.

recognition tuning

The activity of configuring the ASR's settings to optimize recognition accuracy and processing speed.

second orality

Spoken discourse that is a mere vocalization of text, written primarily to be read. A news anchor reading the news and sticking to the script, reading full sentences and whole paragraphs, is communicating through second orality. In contrast, *primary orality* refers to natural, verbal expressions that are spoken naturally and spontaneously, not written in preparation.

semantics

In linguistics, one of the three main branches of inquiry, the other two being *syntax* and *pragmatics* (*see terms*), that is concerned with the meaning of utterances. Note that the meaning semantics deals with is the nonsocial meaning that pragmatics focuses on. So, if a child tells their parent, "I'm hungry," the semantic meaning of the child's utterance is a declarative phrase describing the hunger state of the child. But the child probably also spoke it primarily to communicate a request for food. The latter meaning is the pragmatic meaning—in this case, the main thing the child intended to communicate.

signifier

In interaction design, this is any marker, visual or audio, that explicitly communicates the expected behavior from a person. A sign on a door that reads "Push to open" is a signifier. In contrast, the flat surface of the door is the affordance that communicates, by the fact of its shape, what the user can do (push open the door).

skeuomorphism

An instance of software or hardware mimicking its real-world counterpart. A timer that looks like a lifelike, three-dimensional emptying hourglass would be a skeuomorphism. In voice first, a skeuomorphism could refer to a full greeting spoken by the voicebot—for instance, "Thank you for calling Gordon and Singer," instead of the less human-sounding "[*chime*] Gordon and Singer."

speech act

In linguistics, a speech act is an utterance that only delivers some information but also performs an action. For instance, "Please come in" is both an instruction (please enter through this door and come from outside to inside) and an invitation with potentially many nonlinguistic implications—for instance, legal implications, given that uttering the words was an invitation; the person who acted upon the invitation can no longer be considered trespassing if they enter in reaction to the extended invitation.

syntax

In linguistics, one of the three main branches of inquiry, with the other two being *semantics* and *pragmatics (see terms)*, that is concerned with the grammatical rules and structures that enable the systematic creation of coherent sentences.

tapering prompts

A technique used to shorten prompts and avoid needless repetition. For instance, instead of saying "IBM is trading at 52.15 dollars, up 1.2. Microsoft is trading at 67.51 dollars, up 0.7. Apple is trading at 37.78 dollars, up 2.67," the voicebot could say "IBM is trading at 52.15 dollars, up 1.2; Microsoft at 67.51, up 0.7; and Apple at 37.78, up 2.67."

Wizard of Oz testing

The exercise of testing out a VUI by having one person play the voicebot and another person play the human. The purpose is to evaluate the usability of the interface before any software implementation work begins.

References

Austin, John L. *How to Do Things with Words*. Clarendon Press, 1975.

Balentine, Bruce. *It's Better to Be a Good Machine Than a Bad Person: Speech Recognition and Other Exotic User Interfaces at the Twilight of the Jetsonian Age.* ICMI Press, 2007.

Balentine, Bruce, and David P. Morgan. *How to Build a Speech Recognition Application: A Style Guide for Telephony Dialogues.* Enterprise Integration Group, 1999.

Barthes, Roland. *Mythologies.* Éditions du Seuil, 1957.

Benjamin, Walter. *Illuminations: Essays and Reflections.* Edited with an Introduction by Hannah Arendt. Schocken Books, 1968.

Boorstin, Jon. *The Hollywood Eye: What Makes Movies Work.* Perennial, 1992.

Bouzid, Ahmed. "The Five Feats of the Amazon Echo." *Voicebot.AI*, March 6, 2021. *https://voicebot.ai/2021/03/06/the-5-feats-of-the-amazon-echo*.

Bouzid, Ahmed. "The Five Scandals of Amazon Alexa and Google Assistant." Opus Research, March 9, 2021. *https://opusresearch.net/wordpress/2021/03/09/the-five-scandals-of-amazon-alexa-and-google-assistant*.

Bouzid, Ahmed. "Why Voicebots Continue to Disappoint Us." *CMSWire*, October 12, 2021. *https://www.cmswire.com/digital-experience/why-voicebots-continue-to-disappoint-us*.

Bouzid, Ahmed. "Why VUI Design Is Harder Than GUI Design." In *VUI Visions*, edited by William Meisel, 17–21. TMA Associates, 2006.

Boyce, Susan J. "Natural Spoken Dialogue Systems for Telephony Applications." *Communications of the ACM* 43, no. 9 (2000): 29–34.

Brown, C. Marlin. *Human-Computer Interface Design Guidelines*. Ablex, 1988.

Coates, Del. *Watches Tell More Than Time: Product Design, Information, and the Quest for Elegance*. McGraw-Hill, 2002.

Cohen, Michael H. et al. *Voice User Interface Design*. Addison-Wesley, 2004.

Cooper, Alan. *About Face: The Essentials of User Interface Design*. Hungry Minds, 1995.

Copland, Aaron. *What to Listen For in Music*. McGraw-Hill, 1939.

Crossman, William. *VIVO [Voice-In/Voice-Out]: The Coming Age of Talking Computers*. Regent Press, 2004.

Csikszentmihalyi, Mihaly. *Flow: The Psychology of Optimal Experience*. Harper Perennial Modern Classics, 2008.

Csikszentmihalyi, Mihaly, and Eugene Rochberg-Halton. *The Meaning of Things: Domestic Symbols and the Self*. Cambridge University Press, 1981.

Dahl, Deborah A. "The W3C Multimodal Architecture and Interfaces Standard." *Journal on Multimodal User Interfaces* (November 2013): 171–182.

Davis, Wayne. *Implicature: Intention, Convention, and Principle in the Failure of Gricean Theory.* Cambridge University Press, 1998.

Deibel, Diana, and Rebecca Evanhoe. *Conversations with Things: UX Design for Chat and Voice.* Rosenfeld, 2021.

Deleuze, Gilles. *Difference and Repetition.* Columbia University Press, 1968.

Deleuze, Gilles, and Felix Guattari. *A Thousand Plateaus: Capitalism and Schizophrenia.* University of Minnesota Press, 1987.

Denham, Kristin, and Anne Lobeck. *Why Study Linguistics.* Routledge, 2018.

DeSoto, Clinton. *200 Meters & Down: The Story of Amateur Radio.* American Radio Relay League, 1939.

Essex, Andrew. *The End of Advertising: Why It Had to Die, and the Creative Resurrection to Come.* Spiegel & Grau, 2017.

ETSI Standard, *ETSI ES 202 076v2.1.1 (2009-06): Human Factors (HF); User Interfaces; Generic Spoken Command Vocabulary for ICT Devices and Services.* ETSI, 2009.

Eyal, Nir, and Ryan Hoover. *Hooked: How to Build Habit-Forming Products.* Portfolio, 2014.

Ferro, David L., and Eric G. Swedin, eds. *Science Fiction and Computing: Essays on Interlinked Domains.* McFarland, 2011.

Fuller, Steve. *Post-Truth: Knowledge as a Power Game.* Anthem Press, 2018.

Gardner-Bonneau, Daryle. *Human Factors and Voice Interactive Systems.* Edited by H. E. Blanchard. Springer, 2007.

Goffman, Erving. *Frame Analysis: An Essay on the Organization of Experience.* Harper, 1974.

Graham, Marcus G. *Voice Branding in America*. Vivid Voices, 2004.

Grice, Paul. "Logic and Conversation." In *The Logic of Grammar*, edited by D. Davidson and G. Harman, 64–75. Dickenson, 1975.

Guernsey, Lisa. *Screen Time: How Electronic Media—from Baby Video to Educational Software—Affects Your Young Child*. Basic Books, 2007.

Harris, Randy Allen. *Voice Interaction Design: Crafting the New Conversational Speech Systems*. Morgan Kaufmann, 2005.

Hirst, Graeme. *Anaphora in Natural Language Understanding: A Survey*. Springer-Verlag, 1981.

Honebein, Peter C., and Roy F. Cammarano. *Creating Do-It-Yourself Customers: How Great Customer Experiences Build Great Companies*. Thomson, 2005.

Johnson, Jeff. *Designing with the Mind in Mind: Simple Guide to Understanding User Interface Design Rules*. Morgan Kaufmann, 2010.

Johnstone, Barbara. *Discourse Analysis*. Wiley Blackwell, 2018.

Jordan, Patrick W. *Designing Pleasurable Products*. CRC Press, 2002.

Kinneavy, James L. *A Theory of Discourse: The Aims of Discourse*. Prentice Hall, Austin, 1971.

Kotelly, Blade. *The Art and Business of Speech Recognition: Creating the Noble Voice*. Addison-Wesley, 2003.

Krug, Steve. *Don't Make Me Think: A Common Sense Approach to Web Usability*. New Riders, 2006.

Lakoff, George, and Mark Johnson. *Metaphors We Live By*. University of Chicago Press, 2003.

Landry, Simon. *The Science of Conversational Design: Research You Can Use to Design the Best Voice User Experiences*. Simon Landry, 2020.

Leppik, Peter, and David Leppik. *Gourmet Customer Service: A Scientific Approach to Improving the Caller Experience*. VocaLabs, 2005.

Lycan, William G. *Philosophy of Language: A Contemporary Introduction*. Routledge, 2000.

Ma, Weiye. *Connectionist Vector Quantization in Automatic Speech Recognition*. Katholieke Universiteit Leuven, 1999.

Markowitz, Judith A. *Using Speech Recognition*. Prentice Hall, 1995.

Mehl, Matthias R. et al. "Are Women Really More Talkative Than Men?" *Science* 317, no. 5834 (July 2007): 82.

Meisel, William. *VUI Visions: Expert Views on Effective Voice User Interface Design*. TMA Associates, 2006.

Miller, Peter. *The Smart Swarm: How Understanding Flocks, Schools, and Colonies Can Make Us Better at Communicating, Decision Making, and Getting Things Done*. Avery, 2010.

Mitkov, Ruslan. *The Oxford Handbook of Computational Linguistics*. Oxford University Press, 2005.

Moore, Robert J., and Raphael Arar. *Conversational UX Design: A Practitioner's Guide to the Natural Conversational Framework*. ACM Books, 2019.

Nass, Clifford. "Sweet Talking Your Computer." *Wall Street Journal*, August 28, 2010.

Nass, Clifford, and Scott Brave. *Wired for Speech: How Voice Activates and Advances the Human-Computer Relationship*. MIT Press, 2007.

Nass, Clifford, and Corina Yen. *The Man Who Lied to His Laptop: What We Can Learn About Ourselves from Our Machines*. Current, 2010.

Norman, Don. *The Design of Everyday Things*. Basic Books, 2002.

Norman, Don. *The Design of Future Things*. Basic Books, 2009.

Norman, Don. *Emotional Design: Why We Love (or Hate) Everyday Things*. Basic Books, 2005.

Pannafino, James, and Patrick McNeil. *UX Methods: A Quick Guide to User Experience Research Methods*. CDUXP, 2017.

Pearl, Cathy. *Designing Voice User Interfaces: Principles of Conversational Experiences*. O'Reilly, 2017.

Pinker, Steven. *The Language Instinct: How the Mind Creates Language*. Harper Perennial, 2007.

Reeves, Byron, and Clifford Nass. *The Media Equation: How People Treat Computers, Television, and New Media Like Real People and Places*. CLSI Publications, 1996.

Rutledge, Devallis. *The New Police Report Manual*. Copperhouse, 1993.

Schiffrin, Deborah. *Approaches to Discourse*. Blackwell, 1998.

Schiffrin, Deborah. *Discourse Markers*. Cambridge University Press, 1987.

Searle, John R. *Mind, Language, and Society: Philosophy in the Real World*. Basic Books, 1998.

Searle, John R. *Speech Acts: An Essay in the Philosophy of Language*. Cambridge University Press, 1969.

Seeley, Thomas D. *Honeybee Democracy*. Princeton University Press, 2010.

Simpson, Craig, and Brian Kurtz. *The Advertising Solution: Influence Prospects, Multiply Sales, and Promote Your Brand*. Entrepreneur Press, 2016.

Skantze, Gabriel. "Turn-taking in Conversational Systems and Human-Robot Interaction: A Review." *Computer Speech & Language*, 67, May 2021.

So, Preston. *Voice Content and Usability*. A Book Apart, 2021.

Strengers, Yolande, and Jenny Kennedy. *The Smart Wife: Why Siri, Alexa, and Other Smart Home Devices Need a Feminist Reboot*, MIT Press, 2020.

Tannen, Deborah. *Conversational Style: Analyzing Talk Among Friends*. Oxford University Press, 2005.

Weinschenk, Susan, and Dean T. Barker. *Designing Effective Speech Interfaces*. Wiley, 2000.

Wilson, T. P., and D. H. Zimmerman. "The Structure of Silence Between Turns in Two-Party Conversation." *Discourse Processes* 9 (1984): 375–90.

Wittgenstein, Ludwig. *Philosophical Investigations*. Macmillan, 1953.

Wolf, Maryanne. *Proust and the Squid: The Story and Science of the Reading Brain*. HarperCollins, 2007.

Yellin, Emily. *Your Call Is (Not That) Important to Us: Customer Service and What It Reveals About Our World and Our Lives*. Free Press, 2009.

Index

About the Authors

Dr. Ahmed Bouzid is founder and CEO of Witlingo, a McLean, Virginia–based startup that builds products and solutions to help brands establish and grow their voice and social audio presence. Prior to Witlingo, Dr. Bouzid was head of Alexa Smart Home Product at Amazon and VP of product and innovation at Genesys. Dr. Bouzid is an ambassador at the Open Voice Network and heads its Social Audio Community. Dr. Bouzid holds 12 patents in the speech recognition and natural language processing field and was recognized as a Speech Luminary by *Speech Technology Magazine*.

Dr. Weiye Ma obtained her PhD in speech processing and recognition from Katholieke Universiteit Leuven (Belgium) in 1999 and has been practicing professionally in the speech recognition field since 1994. She has held several technical leadership roles at Unisys, Schneider Electric, and Convergys, and is now lead speech scientist at the MITRE Corporation.

Colophon

The animal on the cover of *The Elements of Voice First Style* is a black-necked aracari (*Pteroglossus aracari*), also known as a beautiful aracari or Maximillian's aracari. This multicolored member of the toucan family lives in the tropical and subtropical forests and woodlands of Brazil, French Guiana, Guyana, Suriname, and Venezuela.

In addition to the black neck they are named for, these aracaris have a black head, dark green back and tail, and a red band across their yellow chest. The upper part of the bill, or maxilla, is ivory while the lower part (called the mandible) is black. Both males and females of this species grow to 14–18 inches long and weigh 8–11 ounces. They live in flocks of up to 10 birds, and while they will travel long distances in search of fruits, nuts, and seeds to eat, they do not migrate. Their breeding season lasts from February to August. Black-necked aracaris build their nests in tree hollows formed by rot, broken branches, or even woodpeckers, and lay two to four eggs at a time. Both parents will incubate the eggs for 16–17 days, and the whole flock may help feed the chicks after they emerge.

The Dallas World Aquarium calls the black-necked aracari "a very noisy bird that shrieks constantly." They are considered a species of least concern by the IUCN. Many of the animals on O'Reilly covers are endangered; all of them are important to the world.

The cover illustration is by Karen Montgomery, based on a black and white engraving from Lydekker's *Royal Natural History*. The cover fonts are Gilroy Semibold and Guardian Sans. The text font is Adobe Minion Pro; the heading font is Adobe Myriad Condensed; and the code font is Dalton Maag's Ubuntu Mono.